IN SPITE OF THE ALPHABET

In Spite of the Alphabet

A STUDY OF
THE TEACHING OF READING

by

HUNTER DIACK, M.A.

University of Nottingham Institute of Education

1965
CHATTO & WINDUS
LONDON

Published by
Chatto and Windus Ltd
42 William IV Street
London W.C.2

✦

Clarke Irwin and Co Ltd
Toronto

First published 1965
Reprinted 1965

© L Hunter Diack 1965
Printed in Great Britain by
Cox and Wyman Ltd
London, Fakenham and Reading

CONTENTS

INTRODUCTORY

My aim in this book is to give an account of the development of ideas about the teaching of reading in the belief that a study of what has happened in the past will throw light upon what is happening now.

In putting the book into a logical shape, I found I had two main difficulties to contend with.

The first was the vagueness of the word 'method' when used of various ways of teaching reading. Writers of books on reading usually classify the practice of teachers as belonging to this or that *method*. The most common labels are: alphabetic, phonic word, and sentence. But a method called alphabetic may also be called the spelling method or the ABC method; a method called phonic may sometimes be called syllabic; a word method may be referred to as the look-and-say method, and the sentence method may be labelled the global method. There are some other 'methods' too—the phrase method, the experience-chart method, the story method, the phonic word method, the non-oral method and even the gingerbread method. It was not possible to solve the problem by banning the word 'method' from the pages of the book; it was too deeply entrenched in the vocabulary of reading for that. The alternative was—and it is part of the purpose of this introduction to emphasise this—to try to keep it clear in the reader's mind that each of these methods is amoebic in its power to change shape. There were alphabetic methods, but no single alphabetic method, and the same is true of all the other practices that are called methods. A subsidiary difficulty to this first main one was the fact that often writers on this subject use the term 'method' when it would have been more logical to refer to 'teaching material' as, for example, when a teacher is said to be using 'the phonic method' when she is in fact teaching by an alphabetic method though using books designed for teaching by a phonic method.

The second main difficulty was to make allowance for the difference between theory and practice, between what was advised and what was actually done. For example, Henry Dunn, secretary to the British and Foreign School Society, in his book *Principles of Teaching or the Normal School Manual*, published in 1837, said, 'The principle of dispensing with alphabetic teaching has long been adopted,' and yet we find school inspectors in the 1880s complaining that alphabetic methods were still being used in schools and even in the 1950s, in her investigation into the teaching of reading in sixty schools in Kent, Joyce Morris found an alphabetic method being used in four of these schools.

My attempt to solve this second problem is to be found in the arrangement of the chapters of this book. The chronology is necessarily very loose, but it is there. From the earliest times of which there is any record until well into the 19th century the alphabet predominated; phonic teaching—in spite of word-method off-shoots—dominated the second half of that century and continued into this; word and sentence methods have been the 20th-century orthodoxy. During the past decade or so there has been a strong reaction, in theory at least, against word and sentence methods in their more extreme forms and this reaction is accompanied by a return to the late 19th-century interest in a form of regular spelling as an aid to learning to read.

My concern is with the reading of English, but much of what emerges in the discussion applies to the teaching of reading in any language which in its printed form uses an alphabet. Inevitably I had to pay a considerable amount of attention to the movement of ideas in America, because most of the vast amount of research into reading problems that has been carried on in recent years has been done in the United States. Since in any case many of the books used for teaching reading in English schools originated in America, it would be unwise for teachers in England to ignore the results of American investigations in this field. The important Unesco world-wide survey of the teaching of reading and writing was, it will be remembered, conducted by W. S. Gray, the doyen of the 'Chicago school'.

Long before I had begun the special reading necessary for writing this book I was well aware that I could not write very meaningfully on the subject without paying considerable attention to developments in the United States, but one of the real surprises I had during that preliminary work was to find that for a century and a half there has been a very lively commerce of ideas between the United States and England concerning the teaching of reading. That same Henry Dunn, for example, whom I have already quoted, said that in writing his book he drew unsparingly from *American Annals of Education and Instruction*, edited by the Rev. W. G. Woodbridge of Boston, a journal of which he found it impossible to speak too highly. There is, too, the interesting case of one of Her Majesty's Inspectors in the 'forties of last century expressing regret that the schoolmaster in a small Scottish village had not heard of the 'word method' of teaching reading as practised in the schools of Boston. More topical is the fact that Isaac Pitman's form of 'augmented Roman alphabet' was tried out over a period of years in at least two towns in the United States. So developments in the two great English-speaking nations were so interwoven that neither could be discussed profitably without considerable reference to the other. I hope therefore that this book will be of interest to teachers and educators generally on both sides of the Atlantic as well as in the Commonwealth.

Chapter One

ALPHABETIC METHODS

FROM at least the days of the Greeks until well into the 19th century the alphabet dominated the early instruction of children in reading. The first thing the teacher did as far as we can make out was to teach the child to recognise and name the letters of the alphabet, both capital and small, in alphabetical order. There is evidence that from the 9th century A.D. onwards the next step was the spelling out of pronounceable combinations of letters. What these combinations actually were depended upon what the teacher had available as reading material. In a great many cases and over a period of many years it was a matter of going straight from the alphabet to the Bible. In 1846, for example, one of Her Majesty's Inspectors, reporting on the schools of the British and Foreign School Society, said that until a few years before that date the sole text for all instruction in reading in those schools was the language of Scripture in the authorised version. The pupils learned to read by spelling out and saying the words of the Bible.

The transition from learning the letters to spelling out the words in a connected passage for reading was not always, nor had not always, been so abrupt, however. As early as the 9th century, there existed manuscripts which gave first the alphabet in small letters, then the same in capitals, followed by columns of syllables:

ab, eb, ib, ob, ub	*ba, be, bi, bo, bu*
ac, ec, ic, oc, uc	*ca, ce, ci, co, cu*
ad, ed, id, od, ud	*da, de, di, do, du*

These were followed by the Credo and the Paternoster.

These manuscripts are the direct ancestors of the horn-book which first appeared about 1450. The hornbook consisted of one sheet in a wooden frame covered with transparent horn. The common hornbook in England had the cross of Christ in the top left-hand corner, the alphabet in both small and capital letters, the columns of *ab*, *eb*, *ib* syllables, and the Lord's Prayer in English. The fact that the syllables were in the hornbook is of considerable significance in considering the process by which the child learned to read by this particular form of alphabetic method.

Even the diligent student of the history of reading is likely to get the impression from books on this subject that the pupil who was taught by an alphabetic method learned the names of the letters but not their sounds. This misconception arises from the anxiety of writers on this subject to distinguish between phonic (sounding) methods and alphabetic methods. They emphasise that in alphabetic methods the names of the letters were given and that in phonic methods the sounds of the letters were given and omit to point out that the teaching material of the simple hornbook, to say nothing of the early primer, was designed quite precisely for the purpose of teaching the sounds of consonants when combined with vowels.

Some alphabetic primers went further and gave the pupils three- and four-letter combinations to read such as *con*, *sid*, *ject*. These were not purely nonsense syllables, since some compilers of reading primers chose letter combinations that the pupils were likely to meet later in words.

Many teachers, besides those in the schools of the British and Foreign School Society, went straight from

the naming of the letters to the spelling of the words in
the Bible and in so doing they could be said to be saving
their pupils a great deal of wearisome drill. At least the
drill that they went through in spelling out the words in
the Bible could be seen to have some connection with
reading. Yet the acme of dullness must have been reached
by way of the alphabet during the first four decades of the
19th century when regimented monitors instructed even
more regimented 'drafts' of pupils in the spelling out of
syllables and words.

There had, however, been attempts to lighten the wearisome process of alphabetic learning. In the 18th century,
for example, there was a vogue for the 'gingerbread
method' when hornbooks made of gingerbread were given
to children to encourage them to learn their letters. Prior
brings it into one of his poems:

> To Master John, the English maid
> A hornbook gives of gingerbread,
> And that the child may learn the better
> As he can name, he eats the letter,
> Proceeding thus with vast delight
> He spells and gnaws from left to right.

That 'method' is more likely to owe its existence to a
baker with bright ideas of sales promotion than to any
philosophy of education, however, though it is true that
a similar idea was put forward seriously by Basedow who
did much to spread progressive educational ideas in
Germany in the 18th century. He suggested that pupils
should be given bread in the shapes of letters. It would
not cost much, he argued, because it would not be necessary for any child to eat the alphabet for more than three
weeks.

Basedow's idea of edible letters arose from his conviction that learning is best when enjoyable, but the gingerbread hornbook, if it did not originate purely as a business enterprise, may well have come into being partly through religious associations. The baking of bread and cakes has strong connections with religious observances—unleavened bread, Christmas cakes, hot cross-buns. The alphabet, too, had strong religious associations since letters were regarded as the key to Holy Writ. The cross of Christ and the Lord's Prayer in the hornbook helped to maintain that association. So, too, did the habit of chanting a short prayer before reciting the alphabet. It is hardly likely that the reverence of which the Credo and the Paternoster were overt expressions did not transfer itself to the alphabet. Nor was this association broken with the Reformation. Luther produced a primer suitable for Protestant teaching and, in the very different English Reformation, Henry VIII encouraged the printing of a Protestant primer in which 'Alphabet and Creed became united in one book which became on the one hand the forerunner of the Book of Common Prayer and on the other of the modern school primer'. In the elementary schools of England which, with the exception of the private schools were run by religious bodies, the alphabet, as I have already indicated, was seen as the way to the Bible. Until well into the 19th century in both England and America, the teaching of reading was inseparably associated with the alphabet and spelling, the Bible usually being in the foreground and never receding very far into the background.

Yet the teaching of reading by way of the alphabet took other forms. In 1827, Professor Pillans of Edinburgh, while not attacking the basis of alphabetic methods, i.e., learning the names of the letters, attacked the custom of making the pupils learn the letters in alphabetical order. He described the order as entirely capricious, said that a knowledge of it at that early stage was quite useless and added . . . 'in the ordinary way the child is arrested, and unseasonably detained in the very porch of learning, by being compelled to name, and not to name only, but to learn by heart, a series of letters, which have not one associating tie to bind them in the memory, but juxtaposition. It is stringing beads, as it were, on a thread of sand.'

Pillans proposed that the letters should be taught in groups which he called 'brotherhoods'. The basis of the grouping was physiological – for example, letters which stood for sounds produced mainly by lip-movement formed one 'brotherhood'. So here we have an alphabetic method in which alphabetic order was put aside in favour of what was in effect a 'sound' order. It was alphabetic in the sense that the pupils still began by learning the names of the letters before learning what sounds they individually stood for. But in how many schools were Pillans' ideas put into practice? This it is impossible now to say. They attracted enough attention to be discussed, and mildly rejected, by Dunn of the British and Foreign School Society ten years after they were first put into print and were referred to in an H.M.I. report as an interesting variation of teaching method five years after that, but more than that I cannot say except that Pillans' ideas indicate that during the 'alphabetic era' teaching was not entirely inflexible and that here we have further evidence that in alphabetic methods the sounds of the letters were not necessarily neglected.

Another variation of alphabetic method also departed from alphabetic order in the teaching of letters. Here several letters were taught in one group, then these letters were put into words and phrases to be spelt and read by the pupils. This variation was devised by a Dr. Andrew Thompson for use in his parish school in Scotland. In addition to a primer the pupils had wooden letters. Here is the material for the first lesson:

o m i s x b y   O S B I X Y M
So is. My ox. Is by. My boy, Is so, My box,
I mix, I miss, Six boys, Miss box, O boys.
Is my ox, O my boys. So I miss, By six boys,
My box is, Is my boy so? I miss my box,
By my six boys, I mix my boys.

The choice of letters seems quite arbitrary but Thompson claimed to have chosen these for his first group because they were the letters most *characteristic* in shape and therefore most easily remembered. He also had in mind their possibilities for the forming of interesting words. It was suggested that the reading matter should be worked on and illustrated 'by the explanatory method'–which meant that the words and phrases were to be talked about in such a way as to put them into a meaningful context. The content of the very first lesson obviously gave the fullest scope for the most ingenious application of the 'explanatory method'.

Dunn in the 1830s had little to say about Thompson's idea but enough to show that he was not impressed. 'No attempt appears to have been made at the Sessional School (in Edinburgh) to remove the tedium of this branch of instruction (learning the letters) unless, indeed, an artificial exhibition of the twenty-six letters on a box, contrived by the late Dr. Andrew Thompson, for the use of his own parish school can thus be designated.' James Gibson, H.M.I. for Scotland, however, in his report of 1843, said that Thompson's idea seemed sound, though at the same time he did write as though he really favoured a word method which had been worked out in detail by the American, Worcester.

Sometimes an alphabet method was almost indistinguishable from a phonic method. Here is the description Seymour Tremenheere, H.M.I. gave of a lesson he saw in London. The date of the report was 1842.

They [the monitors] pointed with one hand to the letter or word to be read, and after a short pause, in which time was given for every child to consider the form and recollect the sound of the letter or letters pointed to, they gave a slight signal by a motion of the other hand, when the whole draft or class pronounced the word together. The reason for allowing this pause proceeds from a correct appreciation of the difficulty a child taught on this system encounters in going over in its mind the many steps requiring its consideration before it can determine upon the sound to be applied to the object presented to it. It must first consider the form of each individual letter, then the form they present in combination; the sound of each separately; the sound to be given to the combination, and lastly the manner of giving expression to that sound. The appliances towards teaching the letters were square pieces of wood with letters on each face, formed by the younger class, under a monitor, into various small words, and practice in drawing the forms of the letters on slates . . .

There is here no mention of the names of the letters, only of the sounds, and yet Tremenheere is contrasting

B

this way of teaching with what he calls 'the phonic method'.

In 1837 Dunn in England wrote: 'The alphabet is usually the first subject presented to the notice of a child at school; and a more difficult and tiresome lesson he is never doomed to meet with in his whole future course.' Woodbridge in America, that Woodbridge to whom Dunn admitted owing a great debt, had been saying much the same for some years and it was in that year, too, that Horace Mann, Secretary to the State Board of Education in Massachusetts, described the reading in the schools of that state as 'too often a barren action of the organs of speech upon the atmosphere'.

After his attack on the effects of this kind of alphabetic teaching, Horace Mann went on to advocate the general introduction of a 'word method', that same word method which the Scottish H.M.I. was to recommend a few years later. Persuasive writer though he was, Mann's influence on the teaching of reading in America does not seem to have been very great; he may have given stronger backing to a method already in use in some parts of Massachusetts, but against him was the massive influence of one of the most redoubtable characters in the history of teaching reading–Noah Webster. Webster was not an educational expert; his main interest was in language and lexicography, though he did practise law as well and, astonishingly, wrote a standard work on epidemic and pestilential diseases. Yet he exerted more influence on what took place in American schools and for a longer time than any single educationist ever did, not excepting Dewey. He exerted this influence through a book which every year for over a century was one of the year's best sellers. This book, when it first appeared in 1783, had the forbidding title *Grammatical Institute of the English Language, Part One*. In 1786 the title was changed to *The American Spelling Book*; in 1829 the title was changed again, to *The Elementary Spelling Book*. In the 1860s it became known all over the United States as 'The Blue-Back Speller'. This spelling-book contained a considerable amount of reading matter in the form of fables and sentences and so it is sometimes referred to, and I think quite rightly, as a primer. I give these details about titles to make things easier for any reader who wants to pursue this matter further. In my own reading I found the different names for what was, with few alterations, the same book very confusing.

The great influence that Webster had in America during the 19th century may be judged by the sales of his *Speller*. This book, first published in 1783, was still being used in the first decade of the 20th century. In 1785, it was selling at 500 copies a week; in 1818 the total number sold had reached 5 million; in 1847 the total had risen to 47 million; in 1889, an official report stated that 1,200,000 were being sold annually and in 1900 it was still selling at the rate of hundreds of thousands a year. The grand total is estimated to have been about 100,000,000. This phenomenal book does not appear to have been published in its original form in England, but a modified version was published here in 1856; it made no great impression. In 1964, the original 'Speller' was re-published as a paper-back in America.

Nobody denies Webster's influence, but there is not complete agreement among the experts as to the direction in which that influence worked. E. A. Betts, for example, director of a reading clinic and prolific writer on reading, addressing a joint meeting of teachers and the American Educational Research Association in 1956, said, 'Noah Webster in 1782 [*sic*], revolutionised reading instruction in America by introducing the teaching of the sounds of letters'. On the other hand, W. S. Gray, writing about 'the alphabet method' in the Unesco publication, *The Teaching of Reading and Writing*, stated: 'During the course of its development, it became highly organised and was given a logical basis—as in Noah Webster's *Speller*, which was used in teaching reading in America and of which 80 million copies were sold during the century following 1783.' These two experts do not agree even about the date of publication. On that point, Gray, however, is right and I have little doubt that he is right too in saying that Webster's influence worked in favour of an alphabetic, not a phonic, method and that the particular type of alphabetic method was that in which the spelling out of the words predominated. This does not necessarily exclude the 'sounding out' of words through the letters, but the very fact that the book was universally known as a 'speller' suggests a closer connection with alphabetic than with phonic methods. In 1889 an English H.M.I., reporting on a visit to schools in America, commented: 'The absurd practice of interrupting reading for spelling is discouraged in America.' This state of affairs in 1889 indicates that in previous years the 'absurd practice' was common and there seems little doubt that it was in some measure due to the distribution of Webster's spelling-book in such large numbers.

If all this is so, how does it come about that so well-known a figure in the world of reading as E. A. Betts concludes that Webster's influence lay towards phonics? There were, I think, two reasons for this. The first derives from the habit of regarding alphabetic methods as being necessarily sharply differentiated from phonic methods. Betts writes as though the mere teaching of the sounds of the letters as well as the names was a revolutionary step, but as we have seen, the syllables of the hornbook and of the primers derived from it were there for the purpose of teaching the sounds of the letters. Of alphabetic and phonic methods it can indeed be said that 'thin partitions do their bounds divide'. To what school of thought or practice did the teacher owe allegiance who said: 'This letter is called "ay". That is the name of the letter. Very often it has the sound "a", the first sound of the words *apple*, *axe*, and *arrow*'? Here the teacher is beginning with the name of the letter and in a matter of seconds giving the sound of the letter, the sound of the first letter of the alphabet is being taught before even the name of the second. Is this an alphabetic method or a phonic method? The second reason derives from the fact that there is a natural tendency to assume that when a writer or propagandist is successful his success has been along the lines he himself intended. There was no doubt about what Webster intended. He put the matter quite clearly in his preface: he set out to devise an arrangement of English words which would most easily show what he called 'the powers of the letters' and he defined letters as 'the marks of sounds'. 'Among the defects and absurdities found in books of this kind hitherto published,' he wrote, 'we may rank the want of a thorough investigation of the sounds of the English language and the powers of the several letters –the promiscuous arrangement of words in the same table

. . .' But the children were to learn the sounds through spelling–and spelling out the words continued as an intrinsic part of the teaching of reading in large numbers of schools well through the 19th century in spite of a considerable amount of criticism. Bulwer Lytton in his novel, *The Caxtons*, published in 1849, made one of the characters say:

A more lying, roundabout, puzzle-headed delusion than that by which we confuse the clear instincts of truth in our accursed system of spelling was never concocted by the father of falsehood. For instance, take the monosyllable 'cat'. What a brazen forehead you must have when you say, c, a, t, spells 'cat'; that is, three sounds forming a totally opposite compound–opposite in every detail and opposite in the whole–compose a poor little monosyllable, which, if you would say but the simple truth, the child will learn to spell simply by looking at it! How can three sounds which run thus to the ear, *see eh*, *tee*, compose 'cat'? Don't they rather compose the sounds 'seaty'? How can a system of education flourish that begins by so monstrous a falsehood, which the sense of hearing suffices to contradict? No wonder the hornbook is the despair of mothers.

So, alphabetic methods were subjected to many criticisms during the first half of the 19th century. Horace Mann's powerful indictment of them in favour of a word method laid the basis for some experiments with word methods in the United States. In England, during the 1840s alphabetic methods received an official reproof when, with the approval and encouragement of Her Majesty's Inspectors the staff of the Battersea Training College introduced what they called 'the phonic method' into their training course for teachers.

Have alphabetic methods, then, vanished completely

from the face of the English-speaking world? Officially
and semi-officially they did so a long time ago. It is several
generations since the alphabet ceased to shine in the
reflected glory of the Lord's prayer, but in 1949 W. S.
Gray was writing that educationists viewed with alarm
an increase in the use of alphabetic and phonic methods,
and Joyce Morris in a survey of reading in sixty schools in
the county of Kent during the late 1950s found an alphabetic method in use in four of these schools—rural schools
where the teachers had found the method successful
enough and had not thought fit to change.

And what about parents at home? The sales of alphabet
books of one kind or another are large enough to give
every English child three or four to chew, tear or scribble
on during his pre-school years. The presence of an
alphabet book in a home does not, of course, mean that
parents are teaching their children to read by an alphabetic
method, but what interested parent can resist letting fall
such interesting pieces of information as 'Ay for apple'?
There is no doubt either that some parents do indeed
teach their children all the letters of the alphabet and spell
out words for their children while doing so 'ay—pee—
pee—ell—ee apple!' At any rate it is a fairly common thing
to hear teachers complaining that many children when they
come to school know the capital letters of the alphabet
and not the small ones and blaming that on a combination
of parents and alphabet books.

Alphabetic methods have the peculiar distinction of
not having been shown by some manipulation of statistics
to be inferior to all other methods or combination of
methods. They went out before statistics came in—went
out as a recognised modern method, I mean. Since no

method has been shown to *everybody's* satisfaction to be superior to all other methods, there does not seem to be complete justification for regarding alphabetic methods as inherently inefficient. To our highly sophisticated minds some of the reading material produced for the early stages of alphabetic teaching in former days certainly seems quaintly ridiculous. As an example of a sentence to be read by a child at the two-letter stage of reading

If he is as I am he is in

will always bring a laugh from a modern audience, but the absurdities of the reading material of nearly every other method can bring laughs too if removed from the context after being carefully chosen to produce that effect.

The alphabet has come back to us in an enlarged, augmented, initial teaching form, but not alphabetic methods. The claim for the new Pitman alphabet is that any method will work with it. This whole new development is, however, the theme of a later chapter in this book. Meanwhile, before drawing this chapter to an end and going on to a survey of phonic methods, I think it will be pleasant to quote a description of a 20th-century alphabetic method. The description appeared in the correspondence page of the *Schoolmaster* on 27th March, 1953, in the course of some lively correspondence about the Simplified Spelling Bill which had just had its first reading and which was the first big step towards the launching of the experiments with the initial teaching alphabet. The writer of the letter was the headmaster of a junior school in Brightlingsea. He described the method by which he himself had learned to read at five and a half in 1915 and said that his wife had learned by the same method at about the same time but in a different school. So there were at least two schools in England in 1915 that had rejected more modern methods. Here is the method as the headmaster, Mr. W. Wilcox, described it.

First two or three weeks: Daily repetition of the alphabet. A B C by name. Abundance of pictures, shapes and apparatus to aid recognition. Games, competitions, puzzles, etc., but all supporting 'drill'.

Second two or three weeks: 'A is for apple', etc., again with wealth of illustration, but repetition and plenty of it.

Second month: 'A (ay) says *a* (short) in *apple*. B (bee) says *b* (uh) in ball.' Children now using pencil and crayons to practise shapes of letters.

Third month: Begin word building 'a (short) and *t* (uh) make AT,' and so on. The first additional sound 'th' is introduced.

By the end of first term, fifty out of a class of sixty were proficient at reading any sentence like: 'It is his hat,'and could also compose new sentences of similar words.

End of first year—age nearly six—the same majority could read: 'Old man bear put on his coat and hat and went for a walk' and the rest of the book. They could also spell the words.

An essential accompaniment of all this was firm, yet kindly discipline We had to learn or take the punishment. The inhibitions so acquired were nothing compared with the complexes now set up when infants at five and a half and six and a half cannot read a word, and dismally inform their parents: We only played again at school.' . . .

When my eldest son, now about to take his G.C.E., had learned nothing in three months, I taught him in a month. At nine years of age he read *Lorna Doone* and *The Three Musketeers* each in a month or so. That is enjoyment. My youngest boy, now five and a half, was taught by the alpha-

betical method *before* starting school. Without any prompting
or help he has entered up his diary each day this year, today's
entry (14th March) being, 'I have got another Little Brown
Bear book.' This is his daily pride, achieved at the cost of a
few tears last summer.

Chapter Two

PHONIC METHODS

JUST as there have been several methods that can be called 'alphabetic', so a number of different methods come under the umbrella 'phonic'. Phonic methods began to make a substantial impact in England in the middle of the 19th century, but many years before that there had been attempts to get away from the alphabetic names of the letters in teaching. In the last two decades of the 18th century a teacher named Kay was teaching reading by his own type of phonic method and, after twenty years of such teaching, published in Newcastle *The New Preceptor* (1801). In his preface he wrote 'As the chief foundation of all reading depends particularly on a thorough knowledge of the pronunciation of the characters of the alphabet and the method of forming them into syllables. I have in the first part given a copy of the alphabet with the names of the letters after what is generally termed the new method.'

In one of the pages devoted to the alphabet, Kay puts at the top of the page the double letters *ch*, *ph*, *sh*, *th*, and *wh* and appends a note:

'These consonants should be named as single characters to the pupils, thus *ch* should be named as "tsh" in *change* . . .' and so on; he classifies the consonants as 'mutes' and 'semivowels', the 'mutes' being those which 'cannot make a perfect sound by themselves without a vowel is joined to them', e.g., *b*, *d*, *g*, the semivowels being those which make 'an imperfect sound' without the help of a vowel–

f, *h*, *l*, *m*, *n*, *r*, and *s*. Kay's book, however, still contained *ba*, *be*, *bi* syllablisation as a pre-reading exercise.

Another early phonic text is *A Summary Method of Teaching Children to Read* (1817). This was an adaptation by Helen Maria Williams of a French book published forty years previously. In this system, the child learned the sounds of letters and indeed of syllables with the help of pictures—for example, he was shown a picture of a butterfly and told to say 'Butterfly—bur' and thus, it was maintained, learned the sound of the letter *b*.

It was in the forties of last century, however, that a phonic method really began to establish itself in England and this was due to work done at the training college which Kay-Shuttleworth, then Dr. Kay, had established in Battersea. Lecturers at that training college had been experimenting in the village school at Battersea and in some London schools with a method of teaching reading called 'the phonic method' and with the encouragement of Her Majesty's Inspectors were producing a handbook for teachers explaining this method and giving guidance as to how pupils were to be taught by it. Seymour Tremenheere, H.M.I., reporting on this, added a note explaining the method. This note is a quotation from a report on education in Europe by Alexander Dallas Bache, president of a charitable college in America. Odd that an English H.M.I. in describing what was happening in Battersea should make use of a description by an American of what was happening in an orphan school in Germany! Here is the quotation:

The child first draws his letter on the slate and is taught to name it by its sound. When the sound of the letter has been learned, not its common arbitrary name but the sound which

it has in composition, the pupil has made some progress towards
knowing how to form combinations which is the next step,
the vowels placed alternatively before and after the consonant. The combinations are first written on the slate and
then pronounced. The next exercise consists in placing a vowel
between two consonants, which is followed by other simple
combinations. These being classified by careful study, the
child is soon able to compose simple sentences, in which his
ideas are developed, so that the mechanical operation of
writing and reading is interspersed with intellectual exercise.
. . . The written letter being once learned, the next step is with
the printed, and a reading book is not introduced until the
child has felt the necessity of it in his further progress; it is
then a relief and not a task.

Clearly there is little difference between this phonic
method introduced from Germany and that of Kay published in 1801 except that the preliminary work was done
by writing on a slate, not by reading from a book.

As teachers went out from Battersea training colleges
into the schools, they took this variation of phonic method
with them. The method which had proved successful in
an orphan school in Germany was admirably suited to the
charity-based elementary schools in England. No cheaper
system of teaching reading could be devised. No books
were required for the early stages, no paper even—slates,
slate-pencils and phonics did the trick. But the fact that
not even a printed alphabet was required at the first stages
was the only real novelty of the method—nearly everything
else had been in Kay's *New Preceptor* of 1801 and no
doubt in other books and in some schools as well.

Publishers quickly became alive to the possibilities of
phonic methods without slates, of reading without the
alphabet, of reading without tears. The 1850s and 60s

saw a spate of 'sounding out' books on the market designed
for middle and upper-class children. Master Winston
Spencer Churchill, as he then was, learned to read from a
book called *Reading Without Tears* and later recorded that
fact in a few sharp sentences in *My Early Life*: 'Mrs.
Everest produced a book called *Reading Without Tears*.
It certainly did not justify its title in my case. I was made
aware that before the Governess arrived I must be able
to read without tears. We toiled each day. My nurse
pointed with a pen at the different letters. I thought it all
very tiresome.' That book was first published by Hatchards
in 1857, its full title: *Reading Without Tears, a Pleasant
Mode of Learning to Read*. The author's name is not given
in the edition I have. He is described merely as author of
Peep of Day, 'A series of the Earliest Religious Instruction
the Infant Mind is Capable of Receiving.' We are also
given the further information that *Peep of Day*, originally
published in 1833, had sold about a million copies in
England, had gone through several American editions
and had been translated into French, German, Russian,
Samoan and 'many other languages'. The author was
Farell Lee Bevan. The edition in my possession is by
Longmans, Green in 1904—so this book was still selling
in the 20th century. It is one of the most substantial reading primers ever published. When the two parts were
bound together, as they often were, there were 566 pages
of text. The author's failure to enlist the willing co-
operation of young Master Churchill may well have been
due to Mrs. Everest and the nurse not to the book itself
because in the preface the author states that the children
are not to be forced to read but are to be *allowed* to
do so. 'To allow them to tread the path of knowledge,

steps have been cut in the steep rock, and flowers have
been planted by the wayside. Pictures are those flowers–
careful arrangement and exact classification are those
steps.' The four means stated to be used to facilitate the
child's progress are 'pictures, classification, the omission
of irregular words, and above all phonetic names for the
consonants'. The omission of irregularly spelt words is
justified in the following paragraph:

The great difficulty in learning to read our own language
arises from the anomalies of its spelling. Why is the *e* in
bread short and in *bean* long? These irregularities cause the
child continual perplexity and render it dependent upon
memory alone. The reflecting child who argues from analogy
will certainly fall into error, while the child possessed of a
mechanical memory will be more successful. But if–of all
the powers of the mind–the reasoning are the most important,
the system on which reading is taught ought to be one calcu-
lated to strengthen and not to suppress them.

Part One of *Reading Without Tears* contained:

(a) Fourteen pages of letters, both capital and small and
in various type-faces including script. With the introductory set there was a picture for each letter with a
statement linking the picture to the shape of the letter,
e.g., of a swan with an arched neck and the statement that
S is like a swan.

(b) A page introducing the short vowels by means of the
words *apple*, *egg*, *inkstand*, *orange* and *umbrella*, each with
its appropriate picture.

(d) A clear run of fifty-four pages of three-letter-word-
practice with the short vowels.

(e) Forty-three pages of practice sentences phonically
simple words plus the word I–e.g. *I had a cat. I had a mat.*

(f) Further sounding practice through syllables: *ba, be, bi, bo, bu; ab, eb, ib, ob, ub*.

(g) When the pupil reached page 118 he read his first story. It began:

Bill is a big lad,
Bill has a cob,
A cob is a big nag,
Bill can get on his cob.

Titles of books published in the sixties show an increasing interest in the phonic aspect of reading. In 1862, for example, there was published *The Pronouncing Reading Book* in which colours were used to indicate different vowel sounds, very different in detail from the reading through colour methods that have been developed recently but with the same basic idea of using colour to help children over the obstacles set up by the irregularities of English spelling. By 1869 so completely had the alphabet lost its magic, so greatly had it fallen in status that a selling title was *Reading Made Easy in Spite of the Alphabet*. This 'reading easy'–there were so many of them on the market that they acquired this generic name–had one novelty about it: every silent letter had an oblique line drawn through it. This was but one of many attempts to print English in some kind of phonetic print and was a mild example of attempts to modify English spelling to fit the pronunciation. By the end of the 19th century, particularly in America, there was a spate of books which tackled the problem of English spelling by changing the appearance of printed words. There were two types of change: one was to keep the letters themselves and the spelling exactly as they were but to add diacritical marks indicating, for example, whether a *c* was hard or soft, an *a*

short or long and so on; the other was to omit the super-
fluous letters *c*, *x*, and *q* and add enough new letters to
enable the orthodox letters to be used to represent one
sound only.

Attempts to produce an easier spelling in order to make
the learning of reading easier were never even near the
main-stream of thought until the second half of the 19th
century and then they were swamped first by phonic
systems which graded the material according to the
degree of regularity in the written forms of the words
and next by systems that were not based upon letters at
all. Yet the idea of making reading easier by an augmented
alphabet had been advocated now and then for centuries
by men wandering between the two world of linguistics
and education.

Probably the first person who gave serious constructive
thought to this matter was John Hart who in 1551 completed a manuscript called *The Opening of the Unreasonable
Writing of our Inglish Toung* in which he said:

. . . I have opened the vices and faultes of our writing:
which cause it to be tedious, and long in learnying: and I
learned hard, and evill to read. . . . And then I have sought the
meanes (herin writen) by the which we may use a certaine,
good and easi writing, onli following our pronunciation; and
keping the letters in their auncient, Simple and Singular
powers.

He concluded his manuscript by offering to teach 'souch
reasonable men as never knew letter, within the space of
one moneth'.

Eight years later Hart published his *Orthographie* which
worked out in detail the principles set forth in his

C

manuscript and suggested that additional letters should be brought into the alphabet so that English could be spelt consistently. A year later in 1570, he published *A Methode or Comfortable Beginning for all Unlearned whereby they made bee Taught to read English, in a very Short Time, with pleasure*. According to Fries, this was the first book designed to teach the beginning of reading with an alphabet based on the principle of using as many letters as there are sounds in spoken English. A. J. Ellis, one of the pioneers of linguistic study in English published a small book in 1845 called *The Alphabet of Nature* and in that book he gave the names of twenty-seven men besides himself who had devised special phonetic alphabets for the teaching of reading. He himself had collaborated with Isaac Pitman to produce in 1842 a 'phonetic print' which they called Phonotypy designed to teach children to read. This was an augmented Roman alphabet. All the letters of the ordinary alphabet which could be used with advantage were retained and seventeen new letters were added giving 'a fixed character for every sound'.

This system was tried out in schools in America and England. An American School superintendent, George L. Farnham, tried out this augmented Roman alphabet in schools in America for five years and found that few of the pupils became good spellers and suggested that because of the 'two systems of analysis', i.e., the two different ways of spelling 'permanent confusion was produced in the mind'. So he reported in his book, *The Sentence Method of Teaching Reading Writing and Spelling* (1881). On the other hand in *The i.t.a. Reading Experiment* (1964) Downing states, 'Stephen Pearl Andrews of Boston first brought the Pitman type to America and it was the pioneering

teachers at schools in Massachusetts who gave it its early
trials for beginning reading, followed by the transition
from Phonotypy to the standard printed medium. As a
result, the pupils were said to have been 'in several
of the essentials of good enunciation and reading *years* in
advance of most children who had been taught in the old
way'.

Later, between 1852 and 1860, Phonotypy was used more
extensively in an experiment in ten schools at Waltham,
Massachusetts. For the first six to eight months the children
used readers printed in the simplified medium and when they
could read Phonotypy fluently they transferred their code-
breaking skill to reading conventionally printed books. A
report of the American Philosophical Society in 1899 summaris-
ing the result of this experiment claimed that in this six or
seven year test with 800 Waltham public school children,
'The effect upon the school life of the town was very marked
as a result of the saving in time needed to teach children to
read'.

This excursion into experiment with a modified spelling
lay outside the main stream of development, however.
In both England and America the vogue was phonics.
Betts gives 1840–80 as the period during which the
emphasis was shifted to sounding out letters either before
reading anything at all or after learning words by sight in
the primer. He draws a distinction between phonetic
methods and phonic methods–phonetic methods being
those which depended upon various ways of showing in
print the different sound-values of the letters. He does not
mention Phonotypy or the experiments with it in Massachusetts but devotes a single sentence to a similar idea:
'In one of its most extreme forms, this phonetic method

employed "pronouncing print" called "pronouncing ortho-graphy".' This was a reference to work by Leigh who produced a phonetic teaching alphabet that was tried out for twenty years in the schools of St. Louis. Betts's con-clusion about phonetic methods was: 'Elaborate phonetic systems broke down under their own complexities. Adding diacritical marks to an alphabet of twenty-three letters plus useless c, x and q, and striking out letters with slash marks made learning to read more complex and com-plicated.'

The period 1840–80 was in America the period of 'phonetic methods'. Thereafter until 1912 phonics (i.e., the emphasis on sounding out words with no change in the form of the print) was in the ascendancy.

Such then were the main characteristics of the situation in America, but, as we shall see, there were some contrary trends. The reactions against alphabetic methods were not solely on phonic or phonetic lines. The idea of begin-ning with words rather than with letters had been for a considerable time in the air and as this idea developed there also developed a situation in which phonic methods and word methods were regarded as contradictory. The educational world split into two camps.

The situation in England between 1862 and the last years of the century was very different from the situation in America because of the effect in England of the 'pay-ment by results' system. Lowe, the Vice-President of the Education Department, had introduced a strict system of inspection for each class in the elementary schools receiv-ing grants from the Exchequer. The amount of money a school received was determined by the number of pupil-attendances and by the number of successes the pupils

scored in the examinations conducted by the inspectors.
These examinations were in reading, writing and arith-
metic. In reading, at Standard I the test was, in reading
'narrative monosyllables' and, in writing, a test in forming
on the blackboard or slate, from dictation, letters, both
capital and small, in manuscript. The necessity for getting
pupils through these tests effectively prevented teachers
in England from trying out experiments which might take
children away from ordinary print or turn their attention
very far from the letters of the alphabet. Indeed the
inspectors' reports in the late 19th century contain many
grim pictures of sheer note-learning and drill. There are
many instances in these reports of teachers making children
chant through the reading-books sentence by sentence
until they had them by heart; there are complaints that
teachers break off the reading with 'the absurd practice'
of stopping to see if children can spell the words they have
read; there are complaints that alphabetic methods still
exist: 'The *see-eh-tee* style of teaching to read still exists
and the same teachers teach the children to read words not
sentences.' (1888)

The foremost exponent of a phonic method in England
in the late 19th and early 20th century was Miss Nellie
Dale whose most important book, *On the Teaching of
English Reading*, was published in 1899. The Dale method
made considerable demands on the teacher and did not
rely at the earliest stages on books. It is likely therefore
that the method assumed a rather distorted form in many
classrooms because the idea that the very first lessons in
reading require books was by that time well established.
Miss Dale's method was a well thought-out one. Her
approach might well be called 'linguistic'. She was

concerned to give the children a rudimentary knowledge of symbols. It was one of her principles not to put letters in front of children until they had a considerable amount of ear, hand and eye training. They were trained to note how they themselves produced different sounds, to note the position of tongue and lips and had their attention drawn to the part played by the breath in the production of the various sounds of speech. The pupils were made to think about how information is conveyed by means of signs, beginning with a good-bye gesture and going on to the arrow indicating direction. At the preliminary stages, too, there was a considerable amount of hand-and-eye training through drawing. Only after this co-ordinated plan of pre-reading activity were letters introduced. Even in introducing the letters there was thorough preparation. There was no question merely of writing a letter on the blackboard and telling the pupils what sound the letter stood for. On the contrary they were told a story–e.g., about a pig. Then they were to discover for themselves how they made the first sound of 'pig'. They were then shown the letter printed or chalked in blue and were told that *p* is a sign for that sound just as waving is a sign of good-bye and an arrow a sign of a particular direction. They were told, too, that the other letters that stand for sounds made in the same way (i.e., without vibration of the vocal chords) will also be in blue. Along with this instruction went the Dale Tabulating Frame which was where the sounds 'lived'. The 'lip' sounds all lived together and had their own special colour, so too with 'teeth' sounds and 'throat' sounds. All this seems very formal, organised and regimented, but the logical framework was by no means the 'method'.

Through the whole scheme ran a thread of fantasy; the letters were little people who emerged from their homes to make words. There was dramatic representation too. The fusion of the separate sounds into a word was demonstrated, for example, by a group of children standing in front of the class, each child holding one letter of the word and in the right order. At first these children stood well apart and the class made each sound separately. Then they stood closer together and the sounds were pronounced with less 'distance' between them. Finally, the children stood close together and the sounds were fused into the word.

In the main the Dale system followed what had become by then established 'phonic' practice. What we may call the primary sounds of the letters were taught first. Yet the *ng* digraph and the soft *c* were taught some time before some of the less common letters.

The Dale system was a highly logical one. Miss Dale herself believed that children were logical beings. The learning of the mother-tongue, she wrote, stands in the very centre of the child's life when it begins to think for itself. 'It is then that it surprises by its adherence to fact, and its decided preference for what is strictly logical; and, keeping this in view, it will be needful for us to present the beginnings of our subject in as systematic a form as we can.' Having said this, however, she found it necessary to add warning: 'But the child is more than a mere logician. We shall all fail sadly if our teaching does not appeal to the heart of the child, its warm sympathies, its love of fun.'

Chapter Three

WORD METHODS

WHEN Horace Mann described the reading in the schools of Massachusetts as 'too often a barren action of the organs of speech upon the atmosphere' his concern was with the fact that the alphabetic methods he saw in operation did not produce meaningful reading – 'meaningful' in the sense of being connected with word-meanings. The children were concentrating so much on deciphering the letters that they had no attention left for deciphering the meanings of the words, if indeed there were word-meanings to attend to; there certainly were none at the *ab*, *eb*, *ib* stage through which, it is reasonable to say, the children in many of the schools he visited would have passed.

Though he was not a professional educationist, having come to the administration of the Massachusetts system by way of the law, Mann was an extremely persuasive writer on educational topics and behind his persuasiveness lay enthusiasm and considerable insight. It was fitting that his reports were the first publication in the current series of Teachers College paper-back editions of educational classics. In his report of 1838 he had some penetrating things to say about language and learning. I quote some of these in order to give something of the context in which one ought to read his comment about the barren nature of the reading activities he had witnessed in the schools.

Though much may be done by others to aid, yet the effective labour must be performed by the learner himself. . . . The pupil may do something by intuition, but generally there must be a conscious effort on his part. . . . It is the duty of the teacher to bring knowledge within arm's length of the learner; and he must break down its masses into portions so minute that they can be taken up and appropriated one by one; but the final appropriating act must be the learner's.

Children who spend six months in learning the alphabet will, on the playground, in a single half-day or moonlight evening, learn the intricacies of a game or sport . . . the whole requiring more intellectual effort than would suffice to learn half a dozen alphabets. . . . Until a desire to learn exists within the child, some foreign force must constantly be applied to keep him agoing; but from the moment that a desire is excited, he is self-motive, and goes alone. . . . The process of learning words and letters is toilsome, unless a motive is inspired before instruction is attempted; and if three months are allowed to teach a child his letters, there is a greater probability that the work will be done at the end of that time even though ten weeks of it should be spent in gaining his voluntary co-opera-tion. . . . When a motive to learn exists, the first practical question respects the order in which letters and words are to be taught; i.e., whether letters, taken separately as in the alphabet, shall be taught before words, or whether mono-syllabic and familiar words shall be taught before letters. In those who learnt, and have since taught, in the former mode, and have never heard of any other, this suggestion may excite surprise. The mode of teaching words first, however, is not mere theory; nor is it new. It has now been practised for some time in the primary schools of the city of Boston—in which there are four or five thousand children—and it is found to succeed better than the old mode. In other places in this country and in some parts of Europe, where education is successfully conducted, the practice of teaching words first, and letters subsequently, is now established. Having no personal experience I shall venture no affirmation upon this point; but will only submit a few remarks for the consideration of those who wish, before countenancing the plan, to examine the reasons on which it is founded. . . . Children . . . utter words—the names of objects around them—as whole sounds and without any conception of the letters of which those words are composed. In speaking| the word 'apple', for instance, young children think no more of the Roman letters which spell it than, in eating the fruit, they think of the chemical ingredients . . . which compose it. Hence, presenting them with the alphabet is giving them what they never saw, heard or thought of before. It is as new as algebra and, to the eye, not very unlike it. But printed names of known things are the signs of sounds which their ears have been accustomed to hear and their organs of speech to utter and which may excite agreeable feelings and associations by reminding them of the objects named. When put to learning the letters of the alphabet first, the child has no acquaintance with them, either by the eye, the ear, the tongue or the mind; but if put to learning familiar words first, he already knows them by the ear, the tongue and the mind, while his eye only is unacquainted with them. He is thus introduced to a stranger through the medium of old acquaintances. It can hardly be doubted, there-fore, that a child would learn to name any twenty-six familiar words much sooner than the twenty-six unknown, unheard and unthought of letters of the alphabet.

The word method that was in use in the schools of Boston was based on Worcester's *Primer of the English Language* published in 1828. In the preface to that book Worcester had said that it was not perhaps very important that a child should know the letters before beginning to read. He might learn to read words first by seeing them, hearing them pronounced and having their meanings illustrated. Afterwards he might learn to analyse them or name the letters of which they are composed.

In the introduction to this present book I referred to
the fact that I had been surprised by the amount of attention paid in England to events taking place in the world of
education in America. One of the instances was directly
concerned with this early American word method of
teaching reading. In 1843 John Gibson, H.M.I. for
Scotland reported on the schools in the presbyteries of
Chirnside, Dunse and Lauder. The report was published
in the Minutes of the Committe of Council on Education.
In a section on methods of teaching he recommended
certain books that every teacher should procure and constantly study. Among these was *Palmer's Teacher's Manual*
and in commenting on the ignorance of the teachers in
that area about alternative methods of teaching reading he
illustrated Worcester's word method by an extract from
Palmer's Teacher's Manual which was in use among
teachers and trainers of teachers in Massachusetts. Here
is part of the extract:

Worcester's Primer is an admirable book for beginners.
We shall use it therefore as our *First Book*. Commencing with
a child ignorant of his letters, we should turn to page 15,
where we find pictures of a man, a cat, a hat and a dog opposite
the corresponding names in capitals as well as small letters.
The teacher may commence thus:

Teacher: What is that?

Child: A man.

Teacher: That is the *picture* of a man. Would you not like
to know the *word* man?

Child: Yes.

Teacher (pointing to the word): There it is. Look at it
well that you may know it again. Now, do you think you shall
know it?

To this question the child generally answers Yes.

Teacher: Which of these words (pointing to man, dog, cat) is man?

Unless the child has been brought up in habits of attention by his parents, his heedlessness will be apparent by his ignorance of the word; and this will generally be the case. So, turning back to page 15, the teacher can say:

Teacher: You are wrong. See, it does not look like that. You should give more attention. Look at it again.

The Manual goes on to emphasise that *one* word is enough for the first lesson, but more emphasis still is to be put on the necessity for making sure that the child knows what he has been reading about'.

He has not, of course, been reading *about* anything at all; he has been 'reading' the one word *man*, but Palmer is merely rather naïvely emphasising the need to make sure that the child understands the connection between word and thing.

The most minute examination of the child as to what he has read must be gone into at the close of every lesson. No excuse can be admitted unless the house be on fire or tumbling about your ears. Should the teacher find there is not time, the lessons may be made shorter, or fewer given per day. Three a week, with questioning, are of far more value than twenty without.

At the second lesson the child is tested to see if he can still recognise *man*. The word *cat* is now dealt with in the same way except that 'there is no occasion to make further use of pictures for the present'. Thereafter it is suggested that a number of common significant words should be taught such as *dog*, *my*, *dear*. They are to be repeated, in print, in different arrangements until the child can distinguish them perfectly and put them together to make sense.

He has thus the satisfaction of reading—of seeing the use of his learning—from the beginning. To make them still more familiar, he should be set to look for the words in a page where they are to be found, and to copy them on his slate. A word may be added each day; and he should be led to amuse himself and exercise his ingenuity by making as many sentences or parts of sentences as possible of his words, and by writing them on his slate. When he has become familiar with a good number of words and is convinced of the usefulness and pleasantness of reading, he may set to learn the letters. This he will do with interest when he knows that by means of them he will soon be able to learn to read by himself without help.

In quoting this American advice about a word method, that H.M.I. was not specifically advocating the adoption of the method; he was anxious rather that the teachers in rural Scotland should become aware of a variety of ideas about the teaching of reading. He was writing also with his fellow H.M.I.s and other people responsible for education in England and Scotland very much in mind. There are several indications in fact that, although phonic methods were dominant, word methods were used in some areas of England from about 1840 or so onwards. Sonnenschein quotes the testimony of a Mr. Mackenzie, H.M.I., given to the Committee of the School Board for London in 1877: 'A few years ago the reading was not at all satisfactory (in the Finsbury division), and it was found that this was mainly owing to the very general adoption of a look-and-say method of teaching and the use of elementary lesson-books not constructed on correct principles for teaching reading.'

In discussing word or look-and-say methods, however, we find as much possibility of confusion as in the discussion of alphabetic and phonic methods. The term 'look and say' changes its meaning with context. In Worcester's Primer the words the child looked at and said were the most common words and the first seven of them were regularly phonic and all three-letter words. The 'look and say' part of the system was merely a preliminary to the learning of the letters and the pace in the first lessons could be as slow as one word a day. In a pamphlet by a Surrey head-master bound in with the third edition (1903) of the *Teacher's Companion* to Sonnenschein's *Reading in a Twelvemonth* I find that it is recommended that teachers should put certain consonants on the blackboard and teach their sound values by 'look and say'. In his own text, however, Sonnenschein says:

A careful study of the problem of teaching to read, based on the experience of half a century, has shown me that there are three, and only three, solutions to it—three and only three medicines within the cup, however much we may vary the honey on the rim: these are:

1st. The Literal Method; or, Reading by Spelling.

2nd. The Syllabic Method, commonly called The Phonic Method.

3rd. The Verbal Method; or the Look-and-Say System, which teaches the whole word at once.

Here we have a striking example of how confusion may arise. Normally 'look and say' implies a word method, but here we have a headmaster advising the teaching of single consonants by a look-and-say method. 'Syllabic method' is here equated with 'phonic method', and yet alphabetic method primers had pages and pages of syllables for drill-work. All the same there is no doubt that the look-and-say methods that were being complained about to the London School Board in 1877 were word methods.

But what shall we say about the McGuffey readers, the most popular of all reading series ever produced in the United States? His *First Reader* appeared in 1836, his *Second Reader* in that same year and his *Third Reader* in the following year. Carpenter in his *History of American Schoolbooks* (University of Pennsylvania Press, 1963) says that without doubt this was the most successful set of reading books from the point of view of numbers sold that had ever been published. It has been estimated that over 122,000,000 copies (I think 'sets' are meant) went into circulation up to 1920. A quarter of a million have been sold since. It is an interesting side-light that McGuffey himself by his contract was entitled to royalties at 10 per cent. only up to one thousand dollars. What concerns us here, however, is the fact that, soon after the publication of the third McGuffey reader, the publisher of Worcester's word method readers brought a law-suit against McGuffey's publisher charging him with 'over-imitation in the McGuffey second and third readers'. The matter was settled out of court and a few lessons were removed from the McGuffey books. At first sight this might suggest that the word method swept the United States but under McGuffey's name, not Worcester's. But there are other things to be considered; the immense popularity of Webster's spelling-book during the same period suggests that no matter what reading-books they used the teachers of the United States did not in general forsake the letter in favour of the word, and furthermore it must be remembered that even Worcester's word method was a very different thing from the 20th-century method which goes by that name in which difference of word-shape counts so much. In any case it is in the primer, the very first reader, that one would expect the main difference between methods to be seen and this law-suit did not concern itself with McGuffey's *First Reader*.

There seems no doubt, then, that phonic methods predominated during the second half of the 19th century nor that in both England and America word methods were being tried out here and there.

Bumstead's word primer of 1840 and Webb's *Normal Readers* of 1848 are usually regarded as the books which in America carried on the line of development that Worcester had started. Flesch, indeed, in *Why Johnny Can't Read* makes Webb one of the main villains in his piece. Huey had already credited Webb with considerable success in spreading the gospel of the word method and had said that this method had by 1870 been adopted by progressive teachers in various parts of the country.

We have seen that knowledgeable people in England were alive to what was happening in this field in the United States. This does not mean that the incipient English movement towards word methods was wholly inspired by what was happening on the other side of the Atlantic. The French educationist, Jacotot (1770–1840) had earlier advocated a word method and his ideas were discussed at favourable length by Dunn in his *Principles of Teaching*.

It was not, however, until well into the 20th century that the supremacy of phonic method was seriously threatened. The threat became a reality after the publication of the results of certain experiments connected with perception carried out in Germany by German and American scholars.

The psychological rationale of the word method, has been demonstrated numerous times by laboratory studies of the psychology of reading. Cattell's study, reported in 1885, is a landmark. Using the tachistoscopic or short-exposure technique, Cattell found that the average adult reader could in 10 mille-seconds apprehend equally well three or four unrelated letters, two unrelated words (up to about twelve letters), or a short sentence of four words (or approximately twenty-four letters if in words). If the limit for unrelated letters was only three or four, the words obviously were not perceived in terms of letters. The experiment definitely proved that we do not ordinarily read by letters but by whole-word units. . . . The older notion had been that words are read by compounding the letters. That this is not the case was clearly demonstrated by the finding that words can be read when there was not time to grasp all the letters. Words must, therefore, be perceived in some other way. Cattell believed that the cue for recognition was the 'total word picture', while Erdmann and Dodge used the expression 'general word shape'. . . . If we do not ordinarily read by spelling out the word or even by sounding it out in detail, little is gained by teaching the child his sounds and letters as a first step to reading. More rapid results are generally obtained by the direct method of simply showing the word to the child and telling him what it is. What makes learning easy by this method is that the sound of the word is already familiar to the child. This is the real justification of the look-and-say method. (Anderson and Dearborn in *The Psychology of Teaching Reading*).

Anderson and Dearborn's book was published as late as 1952. I quote it unchronologically merely because it states so concisely the position adopted by educationists after those early experiments in perception had been

D

assimilated into the theory of teaching reading. The man who first attempted to show the significance of these experiments, however, was Edmund Burke Huey whose book *The Psychology and Pedagogy of Reading*, was published in 1908. This is a remarkable book. It has long been out of print in one sense; in another sense it has never been out of the publishers' lists since the day it was published. I had read many of the standard American texts on this subject before I was able to get my hands on a copy of Huey, but when at last I did so, I had the impression that I had read it before in a number of editions. There were new names on the title-pages; the references had been brought up to date; some ideas were toned down, but the basic material was all there.

Yet Huey has been hard done by in recent years largely because of the treatment he was given by Rudolf Flesch. Having expressed the opinion that the experiments of Erdmann, Dodge and others and the 'total word picture' or 'general shape' theory were not very influential in the changeover from phonics to word methods, Flesch goes on to say that this change really began (he is thinking of the American scene only) with the publication of Huey's book in 1908. He described Huey as a tremendously persuasive evangelist for the word method, who preached the new gospel 'as vigorously as nobody preached it before or since' and who, 'writing as if in a fever', would raise himself to such flights of fancy as:

It is not indeed necessary that the child should be able to pronounce correctly or pronounce at all, at first, the new words that appear in his reading, any more than that he should spell or write all the new words that he hears spoken. If he grasps, approximately, the total meaning of the sentence in which the new word stands, he has read the sentence. Usually this total meaning will suggest what to call the new word, and the word's correct articulation will usually have been learned in conversation, if the proper amount or oral practice shall have preceded reading. And even if the child substitutes words of his own for some that are on the page, provided that these express the meaning, it is an encouraging sign that the reading has been real, and recognition of details will come as it is needed. The shock that such a statement will give to many a practical teacher of reading is but an accurate measure of the hold that a false ideal has taken of us, viz., that to read is to say just what is on the page, instead of to *think*, each in his own way, the meaning that the page suggests. Inner saying there will doubtless always be, of some sort; but not a saying that is, especially in the early reading, exactly parallel to the forms on the printed page. It may even be *necessary*, if the reader is to really tell what the page suggests, to tell it in words that are somewhat variant; for reading is always of the nature of translation and, to be truthful, must be free. Both the inner utterance and reading aloud are natural in the early years and are to be encouraged, but only when thus left free, to be dominated only by the purpose of getting and expressing meanings; and until the insidious thought of reading as word-pronouncing is well worked out of our heads, it is well to place the emphasis strongly where it really belongs, on reading as *thought-getting*, independently of expression.

There, says Flesch, is word-method theory driven well on the way towards insanity.

Walcutt and Terman in *Reading: Chaos and Cure* are much more moderate in their discussion of Huey, but they quote phrases from the same passage and agree with Flesch that Huey was one of the greatest influences towards word methods in America.

Here, however, is another quotation from Huey's book

which indicates that Huey was not single-tracked in his thinking about reading. In these days of experiment with the initial teaching alphabet, the quotation is highly topical. He is commenting on the 'Scientific Alphabet' used in the Standard Dictionary and promulgated by the American Philogical Association and the American Spelling Reform Association. He suggests that this alphabet should at one time or another be made familiar to all children and then goes on:

Besides giving control of pronunciations in what seems likely to be the most generally used dictionary in America, a knowledge of the Scientific Alphabet familiarises the child with the possibilities and with the great advantages of a consistent system of phonetic spelling. Such familiarity attained in the formative period forestalls prejudices; and it can therefore do much more for a reform of spelling than can any propaganda among adults whose habits have set and whose prejudices are naturally strongly in favour of the continued use of the only forms that they have known.

He then points out that undoubtedly the use of two alphabets will lead to confusion.

But such confusion, he adds, is really to be welcomed by anyone who is interested in our real progress in the use of English. When in doubt, the safer way will always be to use the simpler form, and the more doubts arise, the faster will be our approach to a pure phonetic spelling. It is time that American teachers were certain of the plain fact that phonetic spelling is a goal towards which English-speaking people are steadily travelling, although by various roads, and is a goal that will certainly be approximately reached. It is only a question whether we wish to have the immense advantages of such spelling at an earlier date by planning for it, and by enduring, during a perhaps necessary stage of confused spell-

ings, the almost painful feelings that come to many of us when
we see a word misspelled.

In spite of these sentiments, Huey was still of the
opinion that the Scientific Alphabet should be used by
children only for dictionary work. They were not to be
allowed to read a book printed in this alphabet.

How could Huey on one page suggest that reading
should be so free from the domination of letters that it
was right for a child to read a different word from the one
written so long as the meaning was understood and on
another page argue as though he believed letters so
important as to make a drastic reform on English spelling
desirable? Such apparent inconsistencies are far from
uncommon in the field of reading and most of them are
due to the fact that the process of learning to read is not
in itself a clear-cut one. Huey's self-contradiction stems
from some observed facts about the process of learning
to read. Children will certainly learn to recognise words
before they know anything about letters and they can
become so familiar with the printed forms of words
frequently seen that they can get at the meaning without
ever thinking about letters with regard to those particular
words. The only stipulation is that the words should be
known to them in speech as having certain meanings. On
the other hand even experienced adult readers who are
normally not conscious of letters will depend entirely
upon letters when they meet a word they have never seen
before in print and this is what a child must be doing very
frequently. When he was emphasising *thought-getting*
Huey was thinking of the former kind of word-recognition; when he was writing in favour of a reformed spelling,
he was thinking of the other kind.

A similar contradiction appears in Huey's chapter 'Learning to read at home'. One would hardly expect from Flesch's excerpt that Huey was in favour of teaching a child the letters of the alphabet. But this chapter begins:

'Parents who recall their own primer experiences naturally think of the ABC's; but having heard so much of modern word and sentence methods they are confused as to whether familiarising the child with the letters will interfere with his reading later. It may be safely said that it will not.'

He recommends alphabet blocks, matching the alphabet blocks with the letters on old primer pages that may be lying about, copying the letters, arranging them to form words, and copying words. The proviso is that the child should come to a knowledge of the alphabet only as it interests him and by way of play. In this way the child will not only learn the alphabet but will also come to recognise a number of words. But 'real reading', according to Huey, is achieved only when the child gets the meaning of whole sentences. So with Huey a word method merges into a sentence method having begun with an alphabetic play-method.

I have not been able to find any evidence that Huey's book exerted a *direct* influence upon educational thought in England. Reading methods in this country in the years following the publication of Huey's book were more influenced by the work and thought of the Belgian educationist, Decroly. Nevertheless Huey greatly influenced later American writers and through them in one form or another Huey's book exerted a considerable influence in this country. Since this is so and since the book is no longer easily available, I think it will be useful to give an impression of the whole work.

After an introductory chapter called 'The Mysteries and Problems of Reading' there comes Part I of the book with the general title 'The Psychology of Reading'. Four of these chapters deal with the visual aspect of reading in which there is a full account of the experimental work that had been done up to that date. This was long before the photographing of eye-movements, and some of the attempts to record eye-movements by other means sound very uncomfortable—the attempt by a professor at the University of Rostock, for example, to record eye-movements by fixing to the cornea of a reader's eye a tiny plaster of Paris cup with a bristle attached to it for recording the movements on a smoked screen.

It is salutary to read those pages today; they show how much can be achieved by the most rudimentary equipment. The plaster of Paris cup and bristle were not successful, but when the bristle was replaced by a light tubular lever of celloidin and glass connected to a thin aluminium pointer and when the pointer was connected to an electrical circuit broken at regular intervals by an electrically driven tuning-fork, then a record of eye-movements was obtained on a revolving drum of soot-covered paper, because when the eye paused, a stream of electric sparks from the pointer burned the soot off to a greater extent than did the single sparks along the line while the eye was moving. Those single sparks, however, left traces which served as a time-base, for the tuning-fork ensured that each spark was separated from the next by 0.0068 sec.

The chapters that give an account of such research

work are followed by one in which Huey discusses the nature of perception in reading.

I give these views fairly extensively because this is the best way of showing that what Huey thought early this century was the stock thinking of educators until a year or two ago–and indeed may still be:

HUEY ON THE NATURE OF PERCEPTION IN READING

Readers perceive words in different ways. The variation is not only from one reader to another; the same reader will perceive one word in one way and another in another way. The manner in which a word is perceived will depend, for a child, very largely on how he is *taught* to perceive them in learning to read. Various experiences and associations have been woven in with the appearance of the various word-forms. These experiences and associations determine in part what will stand out most prominently in any given word. Sometimes, then, the total word-form is perceived in general outline, sometimes this or that letter or complex of letters stands out, sometimes the word-length, etc. [the etc. is Huey's]. To perceive an entirely new word requires considerable time and close attention and is likely to be imperfectly done, but repetition progressively frees the mind from attention to details and reduces the extent to which consciousness must concern itself with the process. In the act of reading, in addition to the printed form of a particular word on a page, there are clues of context, imagery and feeling which pre-dispose us to 'see' a particular word; there is a 'set' in its direction which may need few signs to set off the proper perception. The first factors in perception are not usually the total form, word-length, etc., but certain striking 'dominant' parts. The appreciation of total word-form and word-length comes a little later as the recognition is completed at the suggestion of these dominant cues. Yet with some readers and perhaps with all of us for many words, the total form, word-length, etc., seem to characterise the word and are apparently the first factors in its recognition. In these cases the general outline rather than a few particular dominant letter-shapes is the aspect of which we are apt to be most conscious in the total recognition. In such cases the recognition could well be set off by a skeleton drawing of the word showing no particular letter-forms and might occur at distances at which particular letters were no longer recognisable as such. But while this kind of recognition is possible and is many times actual it is not the usual nor universal method of recognition. Erdmann and Dodge made the mistake of thinking that it was. The outline form of a word is an inconstant quantity. Much of our reading is concerned with *written*, not printed, symbols and with them the word's total form is often very different from reading to reading. The constant practice of writing words letter after letter, and the use of letters in abbreviations, etc., tends to increase the consciousness of single letters as they appear in words, and thus to break up the consciousness of total word-form. The school practice in spelling and the synthetic methods of learning to read contribute strongly to the dominance of letter-units in the perception of words. Even in the more pronounced cases of letter consciousness, however, it is perfectly certain that words are not perceived by a successive recognition of letter after letter, or even by any simultaneous recognition of all the letters *as such*; it is certainly a recognition of word-wholes, except when even these units are subsumed under the recognition of a still larger units.

Huey then examines the question of recognising a single letter and finds that even with a single letter there are 'dominant' parts and argues that there is a hierarchy of recognition habits; the recognition of dominant parts of the word touch off the recognition of the total form; and similarly the recognition of a phrase *as* a phrase is achieved by the partial inhibition of the recognition of constituent words or letters in favour of the total recognition of the larger unit. Nevertheless there are continual reversions to older habits, consciousness descending to even the level of letter-recognitions, on occasion, and very often taking account of particular words.

Huey followed that chapter with two chapters on the role of inner speech in reading averring that it is *nearly* always present. Here, too, he shows himself to be very familiar with the research that had been done on this aspect of reading up to that date. His last chapter in Part I of his book is called 'The Rate of Reading'. It has a certain topical interest because it mentions most of the things so much talked about today in connection with 'speedy reading'. Huey himself doubled his own rate of reading by waking up to the fact that his rate was unnecessarily slow. 'Doubtless,' he says, 'many of us dawdle along in our reading at a plodding pace which was set and hardened in days of listless poring over uninteresting task, or in imitation of the slow reading aloud which was so usually going on either with ourselves or with others in the school.'

Part II of the book consists of four chapters on the history of reading and reading methods. In these he discusses various types of communication by means of visual symbols, pictographic and ideographic as well as alphabetic writing.

So, clearly, Huey did not approach his theme in a narrow way. References in some of my previous chapters show that I have drawn now and then from Huey's capable chapters on the history of methods of teaching reading. The section on the history of teaching methods in reading brings him to the contemporary scene and he ends that part of his book by stating that he is now going to describe the methods in general contemporary use or that have much promise or suggestion and that he will also note the present trend of practice among the better teachers of reading.

On Part II of his book I have only one comment to make. It is that in his discussion of alphabetic writing he makes no mention of the fact that the order of letters in a printed word stands (with a few regularised exceptions) for the order in which the sounds occur in speech. *Space*, the surface of the paper, is used to represent *time*–the time-order in which the sounds of the spoken word are uttered. In the pamphlet *Learning to Read* I used the expression, 'a printed word is a time-chart of sounds', to bring this idea into relief. It was, it seemed to me very early in my involvement with problems of reading, an extremely important point. I thought, and still think, that to encourage children at the early stages to recognise words by a variety of clues–total length, dominant features, context clues, and so on—was to withhold from them, or at least make it difficult for them to appreciate one of the essential facts about alphabetical writing, the time-chart aspect of it.

Part III of Huey's book is called 'The Pedagogy of Reading' and is on the lines I have already indicated by reference to the concluding sentences of his Part II. I now summarise his 'Pedagogy of Reading'. I shall do this as briefly as possible, but there is so much in it, as I shall show, that is relevant to the present day that the summary will necessarily be a lengthier than was necessary with Part I.

Huey examined more than a hundred contemporary manuals, text-books, and specific systems for teaching reading. He found that the artistic side had been given far more attention than the method and content side.

The books are often superbly illustrated, in colours or with fine photographs, and the covers and typography are most attractive. Of course these are the features which sell the books when, as too often occurs, the selection of texts is in the hands of persons who have no special familiarity with the methods and needs of the subject concerned.

'Next to the beauty of the primer,' he goes on, 'the most striking thing about at least three-fourths of them is the inanity and disjointedness of their reading content. No trouble has been taken to write what the child would naturally say about the subject in hand.' He quotes, 'Is this a ball?' 'Run, little squirrel, run!' 'I am a big boy. Do you see me on the wall? I will not fall.' 'The early lessons are apt to be composed of sentences thrown together with little more than this of relation between them. Now the child loves a story, loves to get somewhither in what is said . . . and has a persistence and continuity of thought that are constantly violated by such "sentence-hash".'

The first specific system he describes in detail is the 'Synthetic Method of Reading and Spelling' by Rebecca S. Pollard which, he says, has been widely used though it was by then waning in popularity. This method is 'purely phonic, almost arrogantly so'. Huey quotes the author as stating that there must be no guesswork, no reference to pictures, no waiting for a story from the teacher to develop the thought.

In its long 'Johnny Story' which is told to the child section by section, Johnny goes to the country and hears the dog growl *rr*, the frog croak *g*, the train puff *ch*, etc. . . . By songs, pictures, and all sorts of personification these associations are drilled in. The children diacritically mark the words in their spellers and readers; they form words from the letters, sometimes with a rotary machine. . . . There are many rules to be learned and more exceptions to rules. . . . Everything is personified and suited to the child's imaginative interest. The small letters are boys that grow to be men and become capital letters. . . . Each letter is a non-talking baby and the child must be mamma and talk for him. . . . The *c* sound is such as when the fishbone troubled Johnny, and so on endlessly.

Huey gives two extracts from the Pollard scheme. One may be too many and yet will serve to show why Huey's feelings rose to so strong a reaction:

'There are pigeons at the barn, mamma. What letter stands for the sound they make?'
'This one: d = D. It is a sound made by young pigeons. You may outline these pigeons and sound as you print each d.'
'This sound presses the tongue up a little harder than *n*. Try the two together, *n*, *d*, *n*, *d*.'

'I can scarcely hear that sound when you make it.'

'No, you can not. It is, besides, a hard sound to make, but I think it sounds like a young pigeon's cry. As *d* stands for what the young pigeons say, you may just think how those two little fellows will talk when the eggs are hatched. It will be *d*, *d*, *d*, then.'

Huey found the 'Rational Method' by Professor E. G. Ward the most increasingly and deservedly popular of contemporary methods. It was a combination of word, sentence and phonic methods beginning as a pure word and sentence method until a small vocabulary of 'sight-words' [Huey's 1908 expression] was known; the phonic work was 'helped' [my inverted commas] by diacritical marks.

There is a description of how reading was taught in The Chicago Institute and the Francis Parker School, Chicago, which is of particular interest since it has so much in common with what is regarded as 'progressive' today. It is indeed the 'experience-chart' method which, in 1955, Flesch described as the latest gospel! The children learned to read as they learned to talk, 'from a desire to find out or tell something'. Learning to read, from the child's point of view is incidental to other things he is interested in. After performing some experiment, or perhaps after working in the garden or observing things in nature the children gather to tell what has been done, and the teacher writes their statements on the board. They read and correct their own statements, and often these are printed by some of the older children and returned as a printed story of what has happened. The child can read these, knowing the gist of it already. . . . 'The child's reading vocabulary is allowed to grow with his experience. As a new word is used in a discussion about garden soils, the word is written on the blackboard and is pointed to, but not spoken, when used later. Its visual form is thus impressed by use. The child may make a little index dictionary of these new words. Diacritical marks are not used appreciably until the third grade, and they are learned then to permit the use of the dictionary. Some work is done in phonics, but this is entirely distinct from reading. The purpose in phonics is to teach the child to associate certain sounds with certain forms, and also to "strengthen his vocal organs," and so lead to "clear enunciation and good pronunciation".'

In a chapter on contemporary opinion about the teaching of reading, Huey spends most of his time on the ideas of Professors Dewey and Patrick of Columbia and Iowa Universities respectively, because he regards the opinions of these two well-known writers as representative of the best modern thought upon the whole matter. It is hardly necessary for me to point out that Dewey's opinions on any educational topic are of significance in the history of educational practice in this country; they were of significance in most European countries. The ideas that Huey fastens on from both these professors is of special interest, and particularly their main point—that the teaching of reading should be postponed until much later than had normally been accepted. This idea had been put forward some years before Huey's book was published and had been taken up with some enthusiasm in England in the 1890s because we read in an inspector's report, 1899: 'The crusade against all teaching of the art of reading until a child is six or seven has so weakened down as to have well-nigh ceased to exist.' But it had not ceased permanently. It came back with renewed strength many years later with the concept of 'reading readiness' and in America it became enshrined in the literature of this subject in the phrase 'delay as a teaching technique' (Anderson and Dearborn). Dewey's view was more extreme than anything that came near serious acceptance in this country. He regarded the age of eight as early enough for anything more than an incidental attention to visual and written language-form. The fetish of Greek was passing, he said, but the fetish of English remained, that the first three years of school are to be given largely to reading and a little number work, but the child is motor at the period when we teach him to read and must not do the passive thing too much. Patrick went further and questioned whether a child should learn to read and write before the age of ten.

Huey agreed with Dewey and Patrick that there would be little loss and often much gain if the child did not read much until his eighth year or later. The elementary school course would have to be changed so that reading and writing would not be taught for their own sakes in the earlier years; the habits of spoken language would be well formed before much reading was attempted; the work of the new curriculum would first develop a desire to read and to read for meanings. At the same time, he admitted, children were at the moment expected to know the rudiments of the art of reading by the age of eight. So, somewhat reluctantly, he put forward suggestions about the teaching of reading in schools. He prefaced these suggestions, however, with a chapter on learning to read at home because it had often been observed–Dewey in fact had mentioned this–that the best readers were those children who had learned at home. Neither Dewey nor Huey commented on the conflict between the fact that children learned to read at home and the belief that children were not ready to learn to read—for physiological reasons in part—until the age of eight.

I have already mentioned Huey's recommendation that the alphabet might be learned by play with alphabet blocks, copying the letters and so on—but that is quickly superseded by *words* theoretically without letters. The child sees words around him and asks questions about them. Then he should be told what these words 'say'. 'He should be told what the whole word or phrase or sentence "says" with no attention to spelling it or dividing it into words even and certainly there should be no attempt to analyse into sounds and letters so soon.' Primers should on the whole be avoided. If one is used any instructions about the teaching of phonics should be ignored.

The natural method of learning to read, says Huey, is just the same as that of learning to talk. It is the method of imitation. The child is born into an environment of spoken language. He hears sentences without grasping their meanings and babbles forth the sounds of letters and syllables without *expressing* any meanings, but gradually and with no confusion, without 'special methods and devices', he catches glimpses of meaning in what is said, a little here and there, and not troubling about the still obscure parts. . . . A few years later, he finds that he is in an environment of books. All of it has at first as little meaning as had the spoken sentences and his scribbling is as little like writing or printing as his early babble was like speech. But he begins to be interested in these printed

E

and written things and to imitate; and the steps from this to facile reading and writing are as certain and as natural as were the earlier ones for spoken language.

So, to delay as a teaching technique there is added the non-teaching method of teaching reading.

But what about phonics? Is there no place for phonics?

'Of course there comes a time when *phonics* should be taught, and carefully taught, but that task may well be left to the school. Besides, the child should long continue to hear far more reading than he does for himself. The ear and not the eye is the nearest gateway to the child-soul, if not indeed to the man-soul.'

Whether at school or at home, the young child is to be occupied mainly with quite other matter than formal exercises in reading until his eighth year at least. The natural basis for a school course at the early stages is the spoken word. Reading may be gradually learned at school more or less as suggested for the home environment. It will be learned as incidental to other activities without harm to the child and with better results than when made an end in itself. The blackboard sentence method is always enjoyed by the children particularly when the sentences are, as in the Chicago school, directly connected with their experiences. Huey quotes with approval from two books that were mostly written by children of the Santa Rosa School in California.

There is no need to hurry the young child into the ability to read every kind of printed matter at sight. The child's reading vocabulary should grow mainly from his daily varying and developing needs of self-expression. Matter which does *not* make such an appeal will long be read with difficulty and will demand phonics and special methods. The remedy is simple; such matter should not be read; its very difficulty is the child's natural protection against what he is as yet unfitted for. New words are best learned by hearing or seeing them used in a context that suggests their meaning, not by focusing the attention upon their isolated form or sound or meaning. It should constantly be remembered that words are functional, and that their main function is to help express a total meaning which always requires or implies their association together with other words. If a word must be learned in isolation, it should always be thought of as saying something of a total thought. The best way to get a reading vocabulary is just the way that the child gets his spoken vocabulary, by having the new words keep coming in a context environment that is familiar and interesting. . . .

It is at this point that occurs the passage, given earlier, that Flesch quoted in condemnation of Huey and the word method.

He comes next to the question of phonics and phonetics and it is here that we find the passage I have quoted about the Scientific Alphabet. Since he says that phonics might safely be left to the school, one might expect him to have some concrete suggestions to make about that in this chapter. But in fact there is very little. He finds himself in agreement with the frequently made statement that phonics has the double purpose of forming correct habits of articulation and of permitting the mastery of new words, but adds that it should accomplish these purposes quite apart from early reading. Studies in the psychology and physiology of speech, he says, indicates that any but the most incidental analysis of spoken language, such as phonics implies, is dangerous before the age of eight or nine. He adds that the necessities of reading do not demand it before the latter age at the earliest. In our unphonetic

English a knowledge of the elementary sounds and of the characters which represent them is not necessary in the actual reading of what is familiar. And there, with the passage earlier quoted about the Scientific Alphabet, is a complete statement of the place of phonics in Huey's philosophy.

The last few chapters of the book come under the heading 'The Hygiene of Reading' and are concerned with such matters as fatigue, width of print areas, and size of type.

The more things change, the more they remain the same. What Huey said in 1908 was being repeated in 1958 with slight modifications as modern and no doubt in 1968 the same ideas will be issued in new bindings and still be labelled 'modern' or 'progressive'. If by that time the initial teaching alphabet is still with us, those same ideas will be more alive than ever because a regularised spelling is itself so clear that confused ideas about the fundamentals of this subject will not matter so very much.

In order to illustrate the modernity of Huey, I quote below from an article by Frank Whitehead, a lecturer in English at the London Institute of Education.

The article appeared in the *Transvaal Education News* in April, 1956. My going to such a faraway and little-known source no doubt requires some explanation. There are two reasons. The first is that this article gives as succinct an account of accepted thinking about reading as I have anywhere seen—and as accepted today as it was in the 'fifties. The second reason is that the quotations from this article set the stage for matters that are discussed in a later chapter. The article, one of a series of three called 'Learning to Read', has the title 'The Principles behind Current Practice' and was written because during a lecture tour of South Africa I had made some challenging criticisms of word and sentence methods. An editorial note explained that a teacher who had attended one of my lectures there had felt so strongly about my criticisms that she had arranged for the series of articles from London.

Here then, nearly fifty years after the publication of Huey's book, are the principles behind the teaching of reading in English schools in the 1950s.

Young children in English schools today learn to read in ways which are very different indeed from those followed by their grandparents fifty or sixty years ago. The changes have come about as a result of a vast amount of practical experiment and scientific research. . . .

Advocates of sentence and whole-word methods of teaching reading have always recognised the need to provide *at an appropriate stage* training in the breaking-down of words into their constituent parts, so that the children may be able, in the end, to recognise 'the sounds of the letters' and build up new words from them. In the last twenty years or so, however, teachers in England (though not, I believe, in Scotland) have increasingly come to believe that the appropriate stage for this training is often a fairly late one. Thus in her book, *Play in the Infants' School* (1938), an account of work in an East London infants' school, Miss E. R. Boyce described how in the children's last six months (i.e. at the age of six and a half to seven) she and her staff 'tried to give them a weapon for discovering unknown words through phonetics'. In a recent pamphlet, *The Improvement of Reading Ability in the Junior School*, the same writer gives excellent detailed advice about training in word analysis, making it clear that she now thinks such work is frequently more appropriate to the first year in the junior school. . . .

Approaches to reading which start with the larger meaningful units of language (either sentences or single words which are given meaning by the context of a classrc om situation) have been based above all upon study of the ways in which young children grow and develop. Thus we have come to realise that children are not just 'little adults' and that the adult's logical order which puts simplest things first may not be the easiest order of learning for the child. . . .

It is interest and purpose that matter most if children of this age are to make sound progress in learning. The keen desire to read, the strong motive and incentive provided by absorbingly interest reading-material, will extend the span of their attention and carry them over all sorts of difficulties. For this reason it is fairly well established now that (although grading and word-control from other standpoints need not be altogether excluded) the words used in early reading need to be chosen above all for their relation to children's most vital experience and activity – the aspects of living which they care about most and enjoy most.

Equally important is our realisation that children's attitudes develop according to a natural and inevitable sequence which we need to study and allow for in our teaching. This does not, of course, mean that all children reach the same development stage at exactly the same age; it does mean, however, that for any individual child there comes a particular time when his maturing abilities are 'ready' to move on to the next stage, and that no advantage is gained *in the long run* by pressing the child to this stage before he is ready for it. (Premature 'forcing' of this kind is, indeed, one of the most common causes of backwardness and apathy later on.) Thus before a child can tackle the beginnings of reading successfully he needs to have reached a certain level of maturity in several directions. He needs, for instance, to be able to talk fluently and listen attentively, and to have had considerable experience of handling books and of being read to from them; his intelligence and powers of concentration, and his acuteness of sight and hearing must have also developed to the requisite degree. Moreover, we now know that children's eyes become able to discriminate whole words before they are able to discriminate between individual letters, and that their hearing develops its power of fine discrimination later still; and this is one important reason why phonics, with its demand for just such fine sensory discrimination, needs to be postponed to a relatively late phase of children's reading progress.

It must be stressed also that our aims in regard to the teaching of reading have become in recent decades more comprehensive and far-sighted. We no longer think that children have 'learnt to read' when they have mastered the mechanics of word-recognition. On the contrary, they see 'learning to read' as a continuing process which goes on throughout the child's school career, and which sets as its goal the power to read with understanding, appreciation and enjoyment–the power, in fact, to recreate as fully and accurately as possible the experience which lies embodied in the words on the printed page. . . . What follows from this enlarged conception of what is involved in reading? In the first place, the emphasis on continuity leads us to value, in the earlier stages of reading, methods of attack similar to those which will be needed by the fluent and accomplished reader at later stages. Thus we regard it as most important that from the very beginning the child should be concerned with 'thought-getting' and not merely with word-sounding; we think it highly desirable that in his attempts to identify new or unfamiliar words, he should at all stages be encouraged to make full use of meaning-clues from the context of what he is reading; and we believe also that it is helpful to future progress to establish from the beginning habits of eye-movement along the line of print which are similar to those used by mature readers. All these considerations reinforce the case for a reading approach which begins with sentences and whole words.

It would be difficult to find a fairer and clearer statement of the 'modern' position in such a brief space. Look
at the works of the major writers in this field in America
and England during the past thirty years and you will
find more detailed information, as, for example, from
individual case-studies, but you will not find any *idea*
which does not appear in Whitehead's article of 1956. Is
there any idea which does not appear in Huey's book of
1908? And who are the 'major writers'? The ones who
have repeated Huey's ideas most often and at greatest
length? Those who have dressed the ideas up most
effectively with statistics? Certainly originality of idea
cannot be the criterion for major and minor writers in
this field were for decades saying the same things. No, a
major writer in this field is one who is most frequently
referred to in the bibliographies as an authority and so we
get the names of: Betts, E. A., Dolch, E. W., Gates, A. I.,
Gray, W. S., Russell, D. H., Schonell, F. J., Vernon,
M. D., and Witty, P. Of these the only purely English
one, Vernon, alone has shown signs of progressive criticisms of the Hueyan ideology, because while in 1937 she
was writing under the domination of the 'whole' theory
of perception, in 1957, in *A Further Study of Perception*,
she had nearly reached the conclusion that the theory
of the 'whole' did not give a valid explanation or description of the processes of perception but was 'rather a one-
sided exaggeration of certain features by no means the
most important in perceiving as we ordinarily experience
it'.

During the half-century or so between the publication of Huey's book and Whitehead's article there had
come, however, the full flowering of Gestalt psychology

and Gestalt theory had an interesting impact upon reading theory. This is a matter best dealt with, nevertheless, in the chapter after next, because in the logic of events sentence methods are necessarily our immediate concern.

Chapter Four

SENTENCE METHODS

To give an accurate definition of 'sentence' is not easy.
The usual definition – 'a complete thought' – merely leaves
you wondering whether you ever had a complete thought
in your life. Fortunately, 'sentence *method*' is easier to
define or describe. Although sometimes grammatical ideas
of what a sentence is, or ought to be, become mixed up with
the idea behind sentence methods, it is nevertheless true
that 'sentence method' may be reasonably defined as a
method of teaching reading whose characteristic is that
the first reading material is to be a group of printed words
that make sense, not single words, and certainly not isolated
letters. The word 'certainly' is necessary in the sentence to
emphasise that sentence methods are the extreme point of
the revolt against letter-based beginnings in the teaching
of reading.

It was in the last twenty years of the 19th century that
sentence methods began to be considered seriously and
the immediate reason for this new development was the
extreme monotony of classroom reading. During the
greater part of the 19th century 'reading' meant 'reading
aloud'. When an inspector tested the reading in the
elementary school, he did so by hearing the children read
aloud. This was not a matter of his personal choice; the
Code of 1862 enjoined him to do so. When, therefore, we
read the inspectors' reports of that period we are likely to
misunderstand many of the references to reading if we
do not insert the word 'aloud' after 'reading'. Again and

again in these reports on the elementary schools of England we find complaints by the inspectors about the monotony of the reading. So too in America. It will be remembered that the main reason for Horace Mann's rejection of alphabetic methods as he had witnessed them in schools was that they resulted in 'a barren action of the organs of speech upon the atmosphere'. In both countries, however, word methods–which Horace Mann looked upon as the remedy for mechanical and meaningless reading–were subsequently found to be producing readers with as little real understanding of what they read as children of the alphabetic generations were reputed to have had.

I think a comment is necessary here, however. There is no *necessary* connection between the manner in which sentences are read aloud and the degree of understanding of them. I may stumble my way through a sentence in a foreign language from word to word, my voice giving no indication whatsoever that I am understanding what I am reading; yet it may be my very concentration on the understanding of it all that prevents me from reading fluently. The true picture of what the inspectors were hearing then is probably that the children habitually read in a manner far removed from the fluency, stresses, intonations and emphases of speech and thereby gave the impression of not understanding what they read. But I have no doubt that many of those who seemed *not* to understand by their way of reading really *did* understand. I have met a great many such instances myself.

The extent to which inspectors were perturbed about the poor quality of the oral reading in the elementary schools of England is very well illustrated in a report of

1882 by E. G. A. Holmes, H.M.I., whose district in that year was Kent. I quote from his report at some length because of the light it throws not only about what was happening in the schools but also because it shows the kind of advice teachers were given. Here we have an inspector of schools, faced with what he sees as a failure of word methods, apparently fumbling his way towards a kind of sentence method.

From the scholastic point of view it is of even greater importance that children should read in the right way than that they should read the right thing, for we cast our pearls before swine when we place suitable books or passages before those who show by their manner of reading that they are utterly incapable of entering into the sense of what is read.

A good style of reading is the product of many factors. Accuracy is the first of these. The child who reads well must know, in any given case, that such and such letters have their counterpart in such and such a sound. Some educationists seem to think that this is the end, as well as the beginning, of reading. They are shocked at the anomalies of what they call our 'irregular notation', and they tell us that if reading is to be properly taught, the flank of this obstacle must be turned by the adoption of the phonic or some other patent system. The phonic system teaches children to translate symbols into sounds, but it does not, and cannot, teach them to read. It is, doubtless, very absurd to tell a child that *see-oh-double-you* spells *cow*, but I cannot help thinking that there is a vast amount of misdirected energy in the current denunciations of this and similar abuses. The anomalies of our 'irregular notation' are not to be denied, but they are by no means the most serious of the obstacles which the teacher, who aims at a good style of reading, has to remove. So far as my experience goes, children can easily be taught 'to know their words', but to say a string of words is one thing, and to read is another, and the former accomplishment is as common as the latter is unhappily rare. . . .

Why is it that, whenever one enters an elementary school during the progress of a reading lesson, the first thing that arrests one's attention is the dismal and unnatural monotony of sound which pervades the atmosphere of the room? The answer is not far to seek. Monotonous reading is a strictly artificial product, and the place in which it is first manufactured is the second or five-year-old class of the infant school.

. . . I open an Infant Reader at random and I find the following sentence: *The child does not know that the dog is fond of cake.* If I read this sentence backwards I put the same degree of stress or emphasis on all the words that it contains. I could not, if I would, do otherwise. It is impossible to make sense out of nonsense, and the sentence when taken backwards is a sentence no longer, but a string of disjointed words. But when I read it forward, I at once begin to modulate my voice, for I am no longer dealing with a string of words, but with a sentence—an organic whole in which each word has its appointed place and function—and if I am to read the sentence aright, I must show that I recognise the functions of the various words by pressing heavily or leaning lightly on each, according as it occupies a prominent or subordinate place by reference to the meaning of the whole. . . . But in 99 out of every 100 infant schools the children are taught to read all the words exactly alike. Not that they are intentionally taught to do this. What they are taught to do is to say each word separately, and say it all together. Now it is clear that if each word is said separately, the same degree of accentuation will fall to the share of each separate word, sense being thereby changed into nonsense, and a sentence into a string of words. Again it is clear that if each word be shouted out by the whole class in concert, the volume of sound which is thus produced will cause the word to vibrate longer than it would otherwise do in the child's ears, and will thus tend to impress upon his senses that monotony of utterance which results from the disruption of the sentence into single words . . . a bad habit will be formed which will speedily develop into second nature, and within a few months at latest the child will have got to believe that the worst possible way of reading is the true and only way, and will instinctively change the whole management of his voice, and not this alone, but the look of his face and even the attitude of his mind the moment he takes his place for a reading lesson and opens his book. . . .

Holmes then gives four rules which, if followed, would in his opinion do much to improve reading.

1. The child is not to be accustomed to read as nonsense what is supposed to be sense. So long as it is necessary to take the words separately *let the right order be carefully avoided*. If you are using reading books, let the words be read backwards. If sheets or cards, let the words be taken in any order except the order in which they come.

2. As soon as you are satisfied that the children know all their words, you may begin to teach them to read. Take the words in their sense order and make the children connect them by twos and threes.

3. You yourself must say the words in the right way – connecting them by twos and threes . . . calling upon the children to repeat each clause again and again until the right way of saying it has been thoroughly mastered, and the different stresses have permanently impressed themselves upon the children's ears.

4. Ask the children questions such as Who kept cows in a wood? A boy. What did the boy do? Kept. Kept what? Cows. Where did he keep them? In a wood. In answering these questions the children will instinctively stress the words aright.

A year earlier than Holmes's report there had appeared in Syracuse, N.Y., a book which gave a much more radical answer to the problem of 'word-calling'. This was *The Sentence Method of Teaching Reading* by G. L. Farnham who had graduated from teaching to the post of school superintendent. His book, first published in 1881 was reprinted in 1886 and again 1895, was widely used in teacher training institutions in the Eastern and Middle West states. I can find no definite evidence of its having had a direct influence in this country. Jagger, who much later, 1929, published another book with the same title as Farnham's, says he found no evidence of any copy having reached these shores—but I am not sure that he looked very far for evidence: he got both the initials of the author and the date of publication wrong and my own deduction is that Jagger's only acquaintance with the book was through a few sentences in Huey's book, which he had certainly read; the fact that Huey gave no initials to Farnham at all lends greater credibility to this deduction.

In his preface Farnham referred to three experiments in teaching method that had been carried out in his area. First, there was a phonetic method—by this he meant not a phonic method but a method which used a regularised spelling—and this had proved superior to the previous alphabetic or spelling method in the speed with which the pupils learned to read but they still read in a meaningless, parroting fashion. Then there was a 'word method'. This had produced better results still in the way of speed of learning, but in the end the reading was as poor as before, the words being spoken as independent units not as parts of a sentence. Note that in America as in England it was customary at the time to make the term 'reading' synonymous with 'oral reading'. Farnham went on;

These experiments and their results, led to further investigation, especially in the line of psychology. From a close observation of the action of the mind, and of the relations of language to thought, it was seen that the unit of thinking is a thought, and therefore that the sentence ought to be made the basis of reading exercises.

He went on to recount that in 1870 a series of experiments was instituted in the schools of Binghamton, N.Y., to test this theory. The results far exceeded expectations in the direct teaching of reading, spelling and writing and led to other results in awakening the mind and influencing conduct which were unexpected and gratifying. It is safe to assume that the problem, how to teach these branches successfully, has been solved.'

I have suggested that Farnham's solution to the problem of mechanical word-calling was much more radical than the four tips to teachers I quoted from Holmes's later report. I think that Farnham was largely misguided by the general direction of his own thinking, yet he did think in an original manner for his day about the problem of reading given his starting point as poor oral reading.

He reached the conclusion that oral reading was not the fundamental process in reading; the fundamental process was silent reading or 'eye-reading'.

It is scarcely possible to exaggerate the importance of correct 'eye-reading'—of the ability to look over the written or printed page, and, with the least possible consciousness of the words used, to fully comprehend the thoughts expressed.

A common process is indicated by the expression, 'reading to oneself'. This means the translation of written into oral language. The reader either pronounces each word so that he can actually hear it, or he thinks of the pronunciation. In either case the thought is not formed in the mind directly through the written language, but indirectly after the written words have changed into oral expression. This process is slow and laborious, it becomes painful when long continued; and its practice will account for the antipathy which so many persons have to reading books and articles of considerable length.

The object in teaching should be to make every pupil an eye-reader—to give him the ability to look directly through the written expression to the meaning, or to at once detect the unknown elements that prevent the accomplishment of this object. . . .

To make the eye perform the office of the ear, and the hand that of the organs of voice, is the problem that presents itself in attempting to teach a child to read and write. The vital point is to so change the function of the eye that it will look upon the printed or written characters, not as objects to be recognised for their own sake, but as directly calling into conscious being past experiences, and so becoming representative of thought. All the efforts of the teacher should be directed to this end.

At this point our education has often failed. The process of translating the written language into speech is so slow and difficult that a large share of the pupils in our schools are condemned to comparative ignorance. The words as they appear have no meaning to them. One who acquires the power of directly receiving the thought from the printed page is endowed with a new intellectual faculty. His eye flashes along the pages of a book, and he comprehends whole sentences at a glance. . . .

When the habit of sight-reading is acquired, oral reading will need but little attention. The oral expression is subordinate to correct eye-reading and its acquisition is largely incidental. When the pupil has the power to take in the thought from the printed page directly, he will have but little difficulty in giving it proper oral expression in the language of the author. The pupil, being under the control of the thought obtained, must read the thought as naturally as he speaks.

F

Farnham then states three fundamental principles:

1. The first principle to be observed in teaching written language is that 'things are cognised by wholes'. The question arises, what is the whole or what is the unit of expression? It is now quite generally conceded that we have no ideas not logically connected with others. In other words, *thoughts*, complete in their relations, are the materials in the mind out of which complex relations are constructed. It being admitted that the thought is the unit of thinking, it necessarily follows that the sentence is the unit of expression.

2. We acquire a knowledge of the *parts* of an object by first considering it as a whole. Repeated recognitions reveal the characteristics of the whole, so as to separate it from other things. We descend from the contemplation of the whole to the parts that compose the whole. Otherwise the parts would be more distinctly remembered than the whole. . . . That words are no exception to this rule is obvious from the almost universal practice of writing out the word and looking at it as a *whole* to determine whether it is properly spelled. . . . The sentence, when properly taught, will, in like manner, be understood as a whole better than if presented in detail. The order indicated is first the sentence, then the words, and then the letters.

3. The distinguishing characteristic of language is that it is representative (i.e., symbolic) in character. Printed words must be recognised but only so as to make the thought expressed the conscious object of attention.

The most notable feature of Farnham's thought is his conviction that there can be a direct link between the printed word and the meaning without the intervention of speech. I am not quite certain what Farnham's answer would be if he were asked to comment on the concept indicated by the phrase 'inner speech'; he would probably have the same attitude that Huey expressed later in the statement: 'Inner saying of a sort there doubtless will always be.' Farnham's idea was, however, that the child should not be conscious of the inner pronunciation of the words he was reading, and apparently this was to hold right from the very start of reading. The big question that Farnham shelves, however, is how 'eye-reading' as he describes it is to be reconciled with the fact that, however irregular our spelling may be, it is still alphabetic–using a system of signs for sounds and sound-order. Yet his idea of meaning being extracted from print *directly* was not by any means still-born. It was one of the prominent ideas in Duncan's *Backwardness in Reading* (1953). Like Farnham, Duncan held the view that the interpolation of speech hindered the acquisition of the thought behind the words.

The extract quoted from Farnham where he writes about the cognising of things by wholes and working from the whole to the parts is, like Huey's statement about the word being more than the sum of the letters and the sentence more than the sum of the separate words, particularly interesting since these words were written long before the rise of the Gestalt school and yet read as though they had come from the pen of a Gestalt psychologist. The fact is, of course, that at the time Farnham and Huey were writing, the preliminary experimental work and thinking that were later to develop into Gestalt theory was already being carried on.

Although I have been unable to find any direct reference to Farnham's ideas in the various reports and discussions on reading towards the end of the century, since his book was so well established in training institutions in America and since ideas travelled so freely in the educational world, I hardly think it likely that his ideas were completely

unknown in England. However, the main influence towards sentence methods in England seems to have come
not from America but from Belgium through the work of
Decroly whose name became very familiar to students in
England training to be teachers. In Decroly's system the
kind of sentence for the earliest stages was the imperative
sentence, for Decroly believed that commands were more
readily understood by children than statements. Commands were also specifically connected with activity which
was an essential thread in the pattern of Decroly's thought.
The sentences were also connected with a 'centre of
interest'–and that 'centre of interest' was the key to the
whole system that Decroly evolved. Thus, for example, in
autumn the centre of interest might be 'fruits' and in such
a case a pupil would be given the command: *Bring me a
pear* and next *Take this knife* and then *Cut the pear in two.*
After the commands were uttered, the pupils were shown
cards each with one of the commands on it and were
required to recognise the sentence as a whole. After they
were able to recognise a few such sentences, they were
taught to recognise words in the sentences and also extracted from the sentences and used as labels for objects
in the room. Then, in a play-way, the sentences were cut
up into words and the words reassembled into sentences.
Later the words were cut up into syllables and the syllables
reassembled into words and finally there was a thorough
study of letters and sounds. In this last phase the Decroly
sentence method was very different from Farnham's, for
although Farnham did indeed 'come down' to letters in
the end he had no use for phonic analysis:

The phonic analysis of words should have no place in
the primary schools. Until the habits of thought reading

and correct spelling are well established, such analysis is positively evil. It makes the child conscious of the oral element in words, and as these do not correspond with the written elements, a double evil ensures: the mind has become directly conscious of language which it should use unconsciously or nearly so; and it introduces a new set of elements antagonistic to the ones used in the graphic expression. The habitual action of the muscles coming from one stimulus, upon which good spelling depends, is directly interfered with by another stimulus which urges to diffcrent results. That antagonism is radical and irreconcilable, and bad spelling must result.

The letters, then, in the Farnham scheme, must havc been learned by giving them their alphabetic names.

Decroly established his first school, a school for abnormal children in Brussels in 1901 and in 1907 he went on to set up a school for normal children and there put into practice the principles he had evolved during the intervening six years. His work attracted a considerable amount of attention in England but it was not until 1925 that a full account of it, *The Decroly Class*, was published in this country. The author was Mlle. A. Hamaide, one of his assistants. By that time sentence methods were becoming popular in parts of England and particularly in London.

In 1929, however, the book by Jagger to which I have already referred was published. He claimed that his reason for writing the book was to dispel misunderstandings that had been spread about and to explain the sentence method to those who held an honourable prejudice in favour of other methods. The reader was not to suppose that the principles advocated in the book were entirely original or perilously untried. The sentence method, he said, had arisen spontaneously in some London schools as a reaction against the mechanical tyranny that phonic teaching had imposed. It was not new as a conception, but the method as practised in London schools was as new as the conception was spontaneous. Phonic methods still 'held the field', however, and he felt it necessary to exhibit their deficiencies, but

the hostility of our attack on phonic methods is not to be interpreted as an attack on infants' schools or infants' teachers . . . Nor should the criticism of phonic methods, and the demonstration that English spelling is not, in the main, phonetic in character, be taken to imply any objection to phonetics, or to the study of phonetics in school. At the proper time, study of the sounds of English, and of the mechanism by which they are produced, is a very desirable part of language-study. The objection is to the premature analysis and synthesis of language, and to the crazy travesty of phonetics which goes by the name of the phonic method.

Those introductory sentences make one ready for some devastating criticism of phonic methods–but they do not arrive. He has in fact only two points to make:

1. When the child's voluntary attention is centred upon the mechanical process involved in reading, it is withdrawn from the meaning of what he reads.

2. Phonic methods need regular spelling, but English spelling is 'largely ideographic in structure'. When English spelling is discussed it is generally assumed to be phonetic in structure; it is regarded as a phonetic failure rather than as an ideographic success.

Jagger goes into considerable detail about English spelling and edges himself into the position where he can seriously state:

English spelling as a means of indicating ideas *directly* [my italics] is a beautiful institution whose disappearance or renovation everyone should lament . . . our system of written words, in structure and in the way that it is used by us, is mainly indicative of the sense; it is indicative of sound in a secondary degree. The written form of each word is associated directly with its meaning and indirectly with its sound, in this resembling the word-ideograms of earlier times. To teach reading ideographically, without the interpolation of sound between written sign and meaning, is therefore in accord with the present character of English spelling as well as in accord with the historical development of writing. It is also in accord with the child-mind, because, as long as the child knows speech only in the concrete, and has not analysed it, he can read pictograms, and no other kind of writing.

Here then we have the extreme view, the final plain assertion that written English is not alphabetic but ideographic. Here is the ultimate denial of the alphabetic principle, the 20th century denial of the significance of letters in printed English.

Now let us examine this ideographic method of teaching children to read English as described by Jagger. The whole sentence is the true first reading matter because it is 'the indivisible unit of thought and language' and, furthermore 'it is all that the untaught child knows and has interest in'. True, these sentences, which have been called indivisible, are for the purposes of teaching broken up into words – but only after the child has learnt to read a large number of sentences. During the period of childhood, however, there is to be no further breaking-up of language; that is deprecated as useless and harmful. Not any sentence will do, of course; the sentences should be such as the child would frame for himself. As the chosen sentences are to be natural, they will be rhythmic, for living speech is rhythmic and they will be pronounced by the child in a proper rhythmic manner. Further, as the sentences are to be adapted to the child's stage of mental development, each of them should contain an image, because the thought of little children of five and six consists principally of images. 'The image aroused by "The cat sat on the mat" (any phonic primer) will not be as vivid as that evoked by "The little grey cat with the velvet paws" (H. Monro, *Milk for the Cat*).'

About the choice of vocabulary Jagger has some things to say. Obviously the words in the sentences must be from the child's own vocabulary, since the sentences are to be such that he might frame himself. But it is to be to the child's intellectual advantage if among the words are some which he has recently acquired, or words whose meaning he knows but which have not yet entered into his normal speech. It is not necessary to avoid long words, provided that the child knows their meaning and can pronounce them. Jagger indeed suggests that a written sentence containing a mixture of longer and shorter words is easier for the child to recognise than a sentence composed entirely of short words; the longer words contrast with the shorter and so give the sentence a more characteristic shape. 'It is less difficult for the untaught child to distinguish between *pretty* and *garden* than between *tip* and *top*; easier for him to recognise "The little grey cat with the velvet paws" than "The cat sat on the mat".'

Did Jagger, I wonder, notice that 'the little grey cat with the velvet paws' is not a sentence?

A useful source for sentences was the children's comments on a picture shown to them by the teacher. The teacher selected a sentence from those comments and wrote it beside the picture for the next morning's reading. In this rather static way of doing things the London schools were far behind the Chicago schools described by Huey who used sentences connected with things the children had *done* not merely looked at. But pictures had another use beside stimulating the children to speak sentences. According to Jagger, in the earlier attempts at sentence-reading the teacher tried to connect printed words and idea directly in the child's mind. This was found to be very difficult for small children, 'because our system of writing is highly artificial'. So pictures were provided to bridge the gap. The picture carried 'its meaning upon its face'; the printed sentence was on the same card. So the sentence and its meaning came to be associated with the conventional printed symbol. On recognising the sentence in its printed form, the child will recollect both meaning and spoken words. Throughout the whole of the process the emphasis has been upon meaning, and not upon the visual form of the sentence, nor upon the sound of the spoken words.

With an unwillingness that he cannot quite conceal, Jagger admits the inevitability of reading aloud.

When a child first recognises a sentence he will read it aloud. That is natural and inevitable, because the signs or symbols of thought (spoken sentences) that he has already acquired in connection with his thinking are needed to reinforce the new symbols of thought (printed sentences) which he is in process of learning. Without the sound of speech to help him he would have difficulty in calling up the meaning of the printed sentences. In doing so he is reading to himself not to others; and in a properly-conducted reading lesson with the class-collection of pictures when individual reading is going on, all the children should be, at this stage, reading aloud to themselves. Such reading is quiet, and in a short time it should become inaudible.

After the child has mastered a number of sentences in conjunction with the pictures, the pictures are withdrawn and the children are required to read the sentences without that aid.

The next stage is the studying of particular words in the sentences 'as wholes'. The teacher indicates separate words in the sentence as she reads the sentence, but not all the words, only those 'of substantive meaning and characteristic form'; she passes over relative words such as *and*, *with*, *to*, *for*, *the*. These occur so frequently that they will be learned without definite indication by the teacher.

The reader who has followed Jagger's argument so far may well be wondering how, according to this method, are the children going to be able to write. To write one needs to know the units of which the printed words are composed—letters. How were these children going to be able to write when they were so persistently being taught that letters as such did not exist? Jagger has an answer to that. At the first stage of writing, the children are to *draw* the words.

From the beginning children should practise reading and writing together, because each will have an effect on the other, an effect varying according to the manner in which it is learnt. If a child innocent of all knowledge of reading and writing, who learns his first sentence in the manner described, is told to write the sentence, he has no resource except to draw it. That is, indeed, the proper course for him to take, because he will know the meaning of what he has drawn. His result will be an ideograph of which he will not know the parts as significant details, and it will probably be so badly drawn that it will be quite illegible in the eyes of others. But he himself, having made it, will be able to recognise and translate it. . . .

Gradually, it is suggested, the rude scrawls of the child's first drawn sentences will become more accurate and by the age of seven or eight he will have developed good letter-form in his writing. It will be 'excessively inconvenient', however, if he does not know the names of the letters of the alphabet. But when he is acquainted with these names, he 'will discern the parts of his ideographs.' Spelling was not to be taught in the infant school nor was time to be wasted trying to eradicate spelling errors. Jagger wraps up his suggestion for dealing with spelling–'if at a later stage spelling has to be made accurate'–in plausible psychological terms, but all it amounts to is that the child is to copy out the words, pronouncing them as he does so and naming the letters.

Such then was the sentence method as interpreted by an inspector of the primary schools of London, a method of teaching children to read as though written English belonged to the same category as written Chinese, with letters pushed wholly into the background and speech allowed to come into the process simply because it could not be kept out.

These ideas perhaps now seem to belong to another world; yet they do not belong to the very distant past. Indeed, in 1955 the Education Department of Transvaal issued to all teachers a pamphlet called the *Global Method of Teaching Reading*. It said much the same as Jagger had said a quarter of a century earlier. A few sentences from the opening paragraphs indicate the line that the Transvaal Education Department had officially adopted:

A child's introduction to reading must be in the form not of a letter, nor of a sound, nor of a word, but in the form of a short easily understood and remembered sentence. . . . On no account must he get the impression that 'reading' consists of looking at or knowing or saying letters or words. The sentence should not be written on the blackboard nor on a chart, but on a flash-card which must be flashed. The child must be taught *not* to look at and say each word separately, but at one glance to see the whole sentence and to say it as a unit. In the old 'phonic method' word recognition is the main aim, and so sentences had to be specially constructed with the words which resemble one another; 'meaning' was a secondary consideration. According to the Gestalt psychology this is quite wrong, because it is far more difficult to learn to distinguish words that have very nearly the same appearance than to distinguish words that do not resemble one another.

Chapter Five

GESTALT PSYCHOLOGY AND THE TEACHING OF READING

Two years before Jagger's book appeared, Koehler, in 1927, had published *The Mentality of Apes*. This was the most readable book any Gestalt writer had so far published and as a result of its publication large numbers of people for the first time realised that there were other psychologists than Freud, Jung, Adler, Watson, and Pavlov. During the 1930s theoretical educationists may be said to have 'gone Gestalt' in large numbers and it was not long before the ideas of the Gestalt school were brought to bear on the problems of teaching reading. To such an extent was this so that anyone who makes his first contact with reading theories through books published since 1935 is likely to form the impression that Gestalt theory provided the original basis for the theories of reading that were rapidly becoming accepted as true and proper. That was my own impression several years ago. When, however, I went into the matter more thoroughly, I came fairly quickly to the conclusion that Gestalt theory did not bring any new ideas to the teaching of reading but rather set into a more imposing framework ideas that had already been widely promulgated. I have little doubt that any reader of this book who knows rather more about Gestalt theory than did that student who began an examination question with 'As Professor Gestalt said . . .' will already have reached the same conclusion. Even so, I feel I ought to go into the matter with a certain amount of detail.

It was in 1912 that Wertheimer, who is regarded as the founder of Gestalt psychology, delivered the Kant lecture in Berlin which came to be regarded as the founding manifesto of the Gestalt school. It is difficult nowadays to look upon the ideas expressed in that lecture with anything like the reverence accorded to them then and for decades afterwards. It is even difficult to give a summary of the lecture without at the same time feeling that Wertheimer is being unjustly dealt with, because the bare statement of what he said does leave one wondering whether he said anything new at all.

What did he say? He defined 'Gestalt' as 'a whole the behaviour of which is not determined by that of its individual elements but in which the part-processes are themselves determined by the intrinsic nature of the whole'. He went on to say that the aim of scientific inquiry ought to be to determine the nature of such wholes. He launched an attack on the kind of thinking which starts from parts and builds up to wholes. He called such thinking 'atomistic' or 'brick-and-mortar' and insisted strongly that it was an unproductive activity of the mind.

Was there in this idea of the Gestalt something new and likely to be productive? It was not the idea itself that was new but the matter of its formulation, the emphasis placed on 'wholeness' and the single-mindedness with which Wertheimer and his followers set out to convince the world that the exploration of the idea of the whole was the path to ultimate truth. After all, thirty years before this famous Kant lecture, Farnham was not only writing about 'cognising by wholes' but was also going on to ask, in the context of reading *what is the whole?*, the important whole which should engage the attention of the teacher of reading at the earliest stages of instruction? And about the same time H.M.I. Holmes was going to considerable trouble to point out that the sentence is an 'organic whole' very different from the mere putting together of the separate parts, while Huey in 1908 was writing about words being more than the sum of the separate letters.

Apart from the idea of the Gestalt itself the Gestalt psychologists laid great stress on the innate organisation of perception. A. F. Watson, a Cambridge psychologist, expressed this idea very clearly in a Third Programme talk:

On the basis of the illusion experiments I have mentioned, together with many others, Gestalt psychologists have felt themselves justified in claiming generally that from infancy we perceive the world in the complex, fully articulated way that we do as adults. That is to say that they regard our perception as being independent of any previous learning: I may be expected, for instance, to pick out the difference between a triangle and a square upon the very first occasion on which I am presented with these figures. What I see will be determined solely by the innate construction of my visual receiving system and the relevant stimuli. This doctrine they expressed by the term 'innate organisation of perception'.

Independent of any previous learning? How previous must any form of learning be before it can be classified as 'previous'? If it took an infant five seconds to distinguish between a circle and a triangle, what was happening during the five seconds? Was he learning? And was his learning *previous* to the final act of discrimination? The hypothesis was full of pitfalls. And yet it was not long before the theory of the innate organisation of perception was given a new form of expression. People began to talk and write about the perception of 'immediate wholes'. Given the theory of innate organisation as the Gestalt psychologists formulated it, it was no great step, after Gestalt ideas were incorporated into the ideology of reading, to turn the phrase 'seeing words as wholes' into 'seeing words as immediate wholes'.

But what did the word 'immediate' mean? There is no doubt that many knowledgeable people took the word in its ordinary time-sense—to see a printed word as an 'immediate whole' was to recognise it instantly. But could a child be expected to recognise any word instantly, the word *parliamentarianism*, for example? The idea was clearly ridiculous in such a case. Perhaps then 'immediate' was not being used in the time-sense; perhaps it meant merely 'unmediated'—that is to say the process of perceiving the printed word was a direct response of the innately organised visual system unmediated by past experience, whether linguistic, perceptual or emotional. But this also implied 'immediate' in the time-sense surely, for if it was not mediated by anything at all why should the process of recognition take any time whatsoever? And so one could go on. Professor D. W. Hamlyn in an article in *Mind* pointed out that a discussion of Gestalt psychology necessarily becomes a discussion of terms and when I wrote at some length on Gestalt theory in *Reading and the Psychology of Perception* I found myself unable to avoid such a discussion and at the same time unable to avoid the feeling that reality was melting away as the epistemological argument proceeded. Here, in this more general book, it may be sufficient to point out how educationists who accepted the concept of 'immediate whole' perception with regard to printed cards and who knew perfectly well that children did not recognise words in either sense of the word 'immediate' managed to resolve the conflict of ideas. They did it by the simple expedient of declaring that teaching methods in reading, if they were to be in tune with Gestalt theory, should aim at helping pupils in their creation of 'word-Gestalten'–that is, pupils should be trained in the instant recognition of words, and the chief means of doing so was the flash-card. The quotation from the Transvaal pamphlet on page 92 shows a further elaboration of this idea.

You may recall that the sentence was not to be written on the blackboard but only on a flash-card 'which must be flashed'. The reason behind this strict injunction was to make sure that the sentence was seen all at once. If the teacher wrote the sentence on the blackboard while the pupils were present, then they would see it part by part as it was emerging from the stick of chalk. If she had it on the blackboard in front of the pupils when they arrived in the classroom, then they would have time to look at the various bits of it. This was thought to be inimical to the best use of the eyes in reading and inimical to the formation of sentence-Gestalten and consequently to speed of reading.

For the reading experts there was no problem of reconciling the idea of training children in the formation of bigger and better Gestalten with the idea of unlearned perception. They were not concerned with establishing or maintaining a consistent theory of the Gestalt but were content with appropriating those parts of Gestalt theory which supported word- or sentence-methods. A vague reference to Gestalt theory was enough. We see this in the

G

Transvaal quotation; in this quotation from Duncan's *Backwardness in Reading*:

We tend to see the whole pattern before we see the parts of it. A young child may recognise the word 'elephant' long before he knows the component letters. It is a distinctive 'word-pattern'. . . . This tendency to see 'in wholes' is emphasised in the Gestalt hypothesis.

and again in *Children Learn to Read* by W. Murray and C. W. Downes:

The whole-word method, which was advocated by Comenius in the seventeenth century, is based also [i.e., in addition to the idea of 'thought-getting'] on the idea that a word is more than the sum of its constituent letters. It has a visual and aural pattern of its own besides being invested with meaning. In recent years the idea has had considerable support from Gestalt psychologists, who claim that we tend to perceive wholes rather than parts of the whole.

The third main plank in the Gestalt platform is indicated by the single term 'insight'–a term to which they gave a special meaning. By the term 'insight' they meant the sudden arrival of understanding–but that is too mildly put. Rather one should say that in one dramatic leap the mind passed over the chasm between blind unawareness and full comprehension. The solution of problems was achieved by a dramatic process of revelation, things suddenly clicked into place. 'Eureka!' exclaimed Archimedes; 'Aha!' cried the Gestalt psychologists, and there is every sign in their writings of a conviction that, with their concepts of the Gestalt, of the 'innate organisation of perception' and of insight, they had discovered things of greater significance than were ever dreamt of in Archimedes' philosophy. 'Eureka!' had to do with a mere fact of knowledge; 'Aha!' had to do with the process through which all such facts were discovered.

The concept of 'insight' was not found very useful by those who were concerned with the teaching of reading and is therefore of no great concern to us here. It is true that in discussing 'insight' Wertheimer found it necessary to launch an attack on orthodox logic and that word and sentence methods were in themselves largely a denial of ordinary logic, but this parallelism was purely coincidental. There was indeed much of the arid and the barren in the kind of logic that Wertheimer attacked, but one does not have to read far in the writings of these Gestalt psychologists before reaching the conclusion that a little of the logic they did not fancy might have done their thinking good.

Was there then nothing in Gestalt theory? One of the readers of *Reading and the Psychology of Perception*, who thought I had been too severe in my criticisms of the theory, insisted that at least Gestalt theory had done education some good by its attack on piecemeal thinking, and this may indeed be true. What is not true, however, is any claim that in the field of reading at least the attack on piecemeal thinking originated from the Gestalt psychologists. And yet, insubstantial though the theory was, its vocabulary came to have some significance in the thinking that went on about the teaching of reading. Terms like 'configuration', 'word-pattern', 'total form' and 'internal characteristics' came to replace the simple word 'letters' in the writings on reading. This is by no means an insignificant change, for when a word like 'configuration' is used, and used habitually, the mental attitude of thinking about printed words as not being primarily composed of letters is reinforced. So Gestalt theory lent its authority to the practice of teaching an alphabetically printed language while paying as little regard as possible to the theory of an alphabet.

One curious result of the 'configuration' idea of teaching reading was to be seen in the design of reading-books to fit the theory. A major attraction of both word and sentence methods had been the promise they held out of release for both teacher and pupil from the narrow restrictions of a regularly phonic vocabulary. The cat was no longer going to be on the mat. Far more interesting material was there waiting to be put together. All that was necessary was to find the words that interested children most, and that was easy; they would be the names of things and actions that the child showed the liveliest interest in. Away back in the early 19th century Horace Mann had said that a child could learn to read twenty-six words in less time than it took him to learn the twenty-six letters of the alphabet and the reason he gave was that the words had meaning and interest, very different from the queer algebra of letters. The average child of five had been shown by A. F. Watts to have a speaking vocabulary of about 2,000 words; others had given higher estimates. So there were plenty of words to choose from—if indeed there had to be a choice. Were not all the words in his vocabulary interesting to the child? Would he have learned to speak them otherwise? What could stand in the way of really interesting and natural reading material?

What did stand in the way was the fact that in spite of all the theorising about 'immediate wholes' and so on, in spite of the undoubted fact that children do recognise words before they know the letters and in spite of the

fact that adults do not pay conscious attention to letters
when they are reading, there is really no argument against
the statement that a group of six letters has a more complicated visual structure than has one letter or groups of
fewer than six letters. Though it might be true that
interest would carry children through the difficulty of
learning to recognise some words while they remained
willingly ignorant of letters as such, it certainly was not
true that they could learn to recognise very easily in this
way the few hundred words necessary for the telling of an
interesting story. Frequent repetition of the words was
found to be necessary and in order that there should be
enough repetition the number of different words had to be
reduced. So the energies of the compilers of reading-books
turned to the problem of designing books with as few
different words as possible, each of these different words
being repeated as often as possible without spoiling the
story. This process became known as 'scientific vocabulary
control'. From the selling point of view it was much
better to say that the vocabulary was scientifically controlled than to say the book contained as few different
words as possible, or to claim that they were designed to
teach children to read by keeping as many words away
from them as possible. For that is what happened.
Theoretically word methods were, at the beginning stages,
letter-less methods; sentence methods were already in
theory, also at the beginning stages, both letter-less and
word-less. You remember? 'On no account must he (the
child) get the impression that "reading" consists of looking
at or knowing or saying letters or words.' Could word
methods also become word-less? 'Scientific control' of
the 'vocabulary load' came very near to accomplishing

that miracle, so near that in one well-known reading scheme the first reading-book has a 'vocabulary load' of only twenty different words—light reading indeed! But were those twenty words really necessary? From one point of view, no. The pictures tell what story there is and if reading is *at all stages* a matter of getting meaning from the printed page, then those twenty words are all of them unnecessary. So the word-less word method had virtually arrived.

This banishing of as many words as possible from the pages of early reading-books was a logical sequel to the banishing of letters from the early stages of reading. It was a logical necessity because children deprived of letter-knowledge are deprived of necessary clues to the reading of words. A statement I found in the general report which a Mr. Cornish, H.M.I. sent to the Committee of Council in 1893 provides an interesting contrast. He was commenting on an improvement he had found in the reading-books produced for five-year-olds. The more recent books had shown a realisation of the need not to include too many different words, for too large a vocabulary was a burden to the minds of young readers. So it was with some pleasure that he was able to mention one book for five-year-olds which 'admirably contains 8,332 words but only 635 different ones'. Mr. Cornish did not give the title of the book and so I am unable to list those particular words. I have no doubt that among them there were many words of different shapes and different lengths; I doubt if every word was interesting to the children; I doubt if the sentences in which the words appeared fitted Jagger's specifications of being attractive, natural, interesting and rhythmic; I expect that they had as little connection with the spoken language of children as the language of Wordsworth's *Prelude* had with 'the speech of humble and rustic life' and I have no doubt that the stories were little more than pretexts for vapid, Victorian moralising. In fact I am not recommending a return to books of that sort. I am merely underlining the contrast between informed opinion seventy years ago and expert opinion ten years ago—the contrast between 635 printed words acknowledged to contain letters and twenty different words in which the letters were theoretically invisible.

Chapter Six

THE PHONIC REVOLT

DURING the decade following the Second World War the learning and teaching of reading was of probably greater public interest in England than at any previous time. The demands of modern warfare are greater than any educational system can meet, for victory, with all its burdens and losses, goes to those nations that can most successfully develop their technological resources and most effectively deploy them dichotomously for defence and attack.

There is, therefore, an insatiable demand not only for scientists at the highest levels but also for men and women who can quickly be trained to handle with some knowledge and intelligence the highly complicated equipment of modern warfare. In acquiring that knowledge—perhaps even in the developing of that intelligence—the ability to read has a vital role to play. In the course of their numerous selection procedures the Services discovered that in a Britain in which literacy was assumed to be almost as widespread as the ability to walk there was a surprising number of men—one did not hear so much about women in this category—who either could not read at all or who could be placed in a new category that went by the name of 'functionally illiterate' which meant that they had not enough skill in reading and writing to perform many of the operations that ordinary readers of newspapers expect to be able to do themselves and are surprised when others cannot—such things, for example, as being able

to read and fill up a form of application for a driving
licence.

Public attention was turned towards these matters also
by the obvious possibility that the upsets of the war might
have impaired the ability in the schools to produce a
satisfactory crop of both full and functional literates.
There was indeed enough public concern for the Government in 1947 to set up a committee whose terms of
reference were 'to consider the nature and extent of the
illiteracy alleged to exist among school leavers and young
people and, if necessary, to make recommendations'. The
first publication of this committee was *Reading Ability :
Some Suggestions for Helping the Backward*. The pamphlet
reported that the Committee had found the eleven-year-
olds of 1948 a year behind the eleven-year-olds in 1938
and the fifteen-year-olds of 1948 twenty-two months
behind those of 1938 in reading ability. The suggestions
the Committee made in the matter of the reading material
to be used gave a clear indication that, so far as any
method of teaching reading could be 'official' in England,
word, not letter-based, methods had the seal of official
approval. The pamphlet listed five main requirements
that were to be taken into account if reading books for
older pupils were to be effective. They should have:
(a) subject matter suitable to the maturity and interest of
older pupils; (b) an approach through whole words and
sentences, with stress on meaning; (c) a light vocabulary
to begin with and a gradual introduction of new words so
that the gradient is easy; (d) many repetitions of the same
material in different guises, the words always being used
purposefully so that pure routine drill is avoided; (e)
illustrations which are simple, but not childish, and which

help the pupil to understand the text. The Committee further testified to its adherence to word methods by stating an important principle that 'the direct link between word pattern and meaning should be rigorously preserved' and stated 'it is generally true that dull children find added difficulty in reading with understanding if they first have to translate word patterns into sound and then sound into meaning'.

The general statement which this committee made about the nature of reading is that:

It is useful to distinguish between the linking up of words with meaning, which is universally regarded as obligatory, and the detailed methods by which children can be helped to read new words. There are many competing detailed methods each with its own supporters and detractors; but it is now generally recognised that no single method is applicable to all children or to all occasions. Sometimes a word will be 'spotted' from its context. Other words may be built up phonetically from the sounds of the separate letters or syllables; though it is worth noting in passing that many of a child's common stock of words do not come under this heading. The phonic method may therefore confuse dull children, if used at too early a stage. Again, in spite of the dangers of establishing mere association of sounds with print, the look-and-say method can be a valuable aid, particularly towards establishing fluency.

In the customary manner of Committee reports, there was also a word to be said on the other side: 'Occasionally a child may find a pure phonic method best of all.'

In 1957 the Committee published another pamphlet, *Standards of Reading* 1948–56. In this they reported that there was on the whole an improvement in reading ability amongst school children between 1948 and 1956 but the 1956 children were still below the standard of the children of 1937, yet 'in any case doubt whether all the leeway has been made up is no reason for dissatisfaction with the progress already made'.

From 1951 onwards, J. C. Daniels and I, colleagues at the University of Nottingham Institute of Education, had been doing a considerable amount of work with backward readers and had reached conclusions different from the official ones about the nature of reading itself, about the process of perception in reading, and about the kind of material most suitable for teaching this basic skill. It was therefore with a certain wry interest that we witnessed official blessing still being bestowed upon theories that as far as we could find out had never been *proved* to be successful and that we were in the process of showing to be inefficient.

In the spring and autumn issue of the *Head Teachers' Review*, 1953, we set out in two articles a preliminary outline of the theory we were working on and a sketch of the kind of teaching material it involved. These two articles gave a cool, calm and, we thought, objective statement of the situation as we saw it and appeared to have the effect such a statement may be expected to have — none at all.

From that quiet beginning, however, there developed a controversy which surprised us by its intensity. But first there came the surprise of discovering that there was a much more widely-spread interest in what we had to say than we had ever expected. The first indication of this came after I had given a talk to a Parent-Teacher Association one Saturday afternoon in Nottingham. In the course of the talk I had said that modern theories of teaching reading had thrown away the alphabet, the very basis of

Western civilisation. This statement was taken up by a reporter and was the key-line in a 600–700 word report in the *Manchester Guardian* (as it then was) on the Monday morning. Some weeks later I was surprised to have handed to me a word-for-word reprint on that report from the *Bulawayo Times*. Later still came correspondence which seemed to indicate that in many parts of the English-speaking world there was an uneasiness about the state of reading instruction.

It was, however, a brief article in the *News Chronicle* that set the spark to the dry tinder. Their educational correspondent had written in moderately glowing terms about modern theories of teaching reading. There was every indication that he thought it a good thing that children and teachers were no longer being bothered by letters or simple three-letter words. The implication that all contemporary educationists accepted word methods without question stimulated me to write and point out that this was not so. The result of this letter was a visit from the correspondent, a discussion between him, J. C. Daniels and myself and another report in the *News Chronicle*, in which our criticisms of word methods were expressed, and a spate of correspondence. Within a few days about 400 letters were received at the *News Chronicle* office. We had about 120. A rough breakdown by the *News Chronicle* suggested that about half the letters were antagonistic to our ideas and the rest sympathetic. Some of the opposition was quite violent in its language. Nearly all the letters that came to us direct were very much in sympathy with what we were saying.

It happened that at that time the *News Chronicle* was considering the publication of a series of current-affairs pamphlets. The series began – and I think ended – with a pamphlet we wrote called *Learning to Read: An Outline of a New Teaching Method*.

While we were writing this 28-page pamphlet, however, still stronger evidence came that our views had set part of the educational world by the ears, for, as a result of the newspaper interview and the subsequent correspondence, the most popular teachers' journal in England, the *Teachers' World* filled its front page with a stirring article by one of its regular feature-writers who added ginger to his article by implying that we were using our position and the name of a university in order to put over upon an unsuspecting public ideas and opinions that so far had not had the backing of any responsible research work. Teachers, he said, had a right to know with what authority we spoke. Our opinions were causing distress among many dedicated teachers and were quite out of line with what responsible educational opinion had come to accept. He went on to explain the theory of the word method rather less calmly than Huey had done about half a century earlier but with little change of idea. There was, it seemed to me, a fair amount of misrepresentation in the article and certainly no attempt to understand the reasons behind our statements. Readers of the *Teachers' World* could not be expected to know all that had gone before and not many of them would have seen the plain statement of our position in the *Head Teachers' Review* of the previous spring and autumn. Therefore I wrote a letter to the editor of the *Teachers' World* in an attempt to answer some of the misrepresentations. This was a mistake, for the editor immediately handed my letter over to the feature-writer who filled another front page of the paper with such extracts from my letter as suited his argument and interspersed them with comments of his own. The misrepresentation was worse than before and the feature-writer was able to emerge from the encounter as the champion of children and infant teachers against the fell plans of two academics who were out to destroy all that was best in modern education. I had not met such treatment in serious journalism before, but in the midst of this tactical defeat it was with some pleasure that I reflected that our *News Chronicle* pamphlet would soon burst upon the interested public and I sincerely hoped that some of the readers of the *Teachers' World* would be in that public.

The *News Chronicle* printed 15,000 copies of *Learning to Read* and distributed copies free at the annual conference of the National Union of Teachers in 1954. It was subsequently re-published by Chatto and Windus, but has long been out of print. Since it is now no longer available I now give an outline of it.

There was a brief mention of alphabetic methods, including the quotation of the two-letter stage sentence: *If he is as I am he is in.* This sentence was used to show how unnatural the language was in those early books and to point out that a short word could indeed be more difficult to understand than a long one; for instance, *as* in that sentence was more difficult to the ordinary child today than the word *television.* Phonic methods were then mentioned with two criticisms:

1. The sounds that the letters *c–a–t* stand for in *cat* are not *ker–a–*ter but the sounds in the word *cat.* To ask a child at this early age to put together *ker-a-ter* and make 'cat' is asking him to do the impossible. The idea is too abstract for the very young child.

2. The vocabulary of the old phonic books was limited in both words and meaning. 'The cat sat on the mat' has become the symbol of dullness in reading materials. Teachers could not remain for ever content with uninspiring, drill-sergeant methods.

By stages there developed the idea that children recognise whole words, if not indeed whole sentences, before they are able to recognise letters or differentiate between them.

If a child could *read* any word by its shape or pattern, without the need to analyse it into letters and their sounds, then there was no restriction on the choice of words except the limitation of the child's interest, understanding and experience. There can be no doubt that, when put into practice, this theory injected new vitality into the work of teaching infants to read. If certain precautions had been taken there would now be very little to complain of about the teaching of reading. But the theory was full of booby traps and a remarkable number of leaders of educational thought stepped right into them.

A brief section about the difference between the reading of the experienced adult and the learning child led on to a statement of three basic principles.

1. In written English, letters or combinations of letters, stand for sounds. We took due note of exceptions like the *gh* of *through*.

2. The order of the letters in a printed word, read from left to right, stands for the order in which the sounds are made. Again exceptions were noted, e.g., the *e* in *came* which modifies the vowel two letters back.

Before we stated the third principle we made the following comments:

Our first and second principles, taken together, are in effect a definition of an alphabet. An alphabet is a system of symbols for sounds and these symbols are written down in the order in which the sounds are made. A printed word is a time-chart of sound. The act of reading is the act of translating those time-charts into the appropriate sounds, the sounds (I should now write 'sound-patterns' or 'blocks of sound') being associated with things, events, or emotions.

Many of the problems of teaching reading come from the fact that there are so many irregularities in English spelling.

We do not advocate a system of simplified spelling, but we see only two ways of reducing the enormous waste of man-power which a chaotic spelling system involves. One is to simplify our spelling; but the chances of this coming about are so slight as to be negligible. The other is to reduce chaos into some kind of order by a careful choice of early reading material.

3. Sounds without meaning are not language.

We stated that these three principles taken together amount to a definition of language written down by means of an alphabet.

This section was followed by a criticism of the idea that children should be introduced to words of as different shape as possible. We pointed out that what a child learns is largely determined by what the teacher places before him or draws his attention to. 'In concentrating too much attention of the *shapes* of words, the teacher is, in *effect* teaching the pupils that letters are not important.' Our basic idea was that in the perception of words a process of *visual* analysis is necessary. The logical deduction was that the *visual* analysis should be into letters not such features as the dots on *i*'s and the tails on *y*'s.

We went on to describe what was actually happening in the schools and argued that 'mixed methods', which were so common in the schools, were a compromise forced upon teachers because of the prevalence of look-and-say books and pointed out how difficult it was for a teacher to teach children the significance of letters from books which *on principle* used such words as 'aeroplane' and 'bicycle' for the earliest stages of reading.

The last section of the pamphlet described briefly what we now call 'the phonic word method' as incorporated in the *Royal Road Readers*. This method is based on the idea that material for teaching reading ought to be designed so as to give the child in as easy a manner as possible insight into the nature of letters. In the scheme the child does not learn the letters in isolation but functioning in words.

In the controversy that dragged on for several years in the Press, the critics of our ideas persistently stated that we were limiting the child to three-letter words and advocating the teaching of reading three-letter words from the first day in school, that we were throwing aside all idea of creative activity and turning reading into a barren drill. Yet in *Learning to Read* the following sentences occurred:

. . . the actual material must be supplemented by the teacher through activities devised to help the children to consolidate the knowledge they have gained. The children should not work at the material we describe and nothing else. Far from it. They should be writing, drawing, looking at pictures, listening

H

to stories and speaking themselves. . . In the infant school the scheme would be wedded to all kinds of activities, and actual work on the scheme should be for short but profitable periods.

The principles which it appears to us should be observed at the very earliest stage of learning to read are as follow:

1. The materials should be well-illustrated 'active' materials.

2. They should sustain the interest of children.

3. They should lead the children, step by step, but as rapidly as possible, to an understanding that letters in words stand for sounds in a certain order and should begin by teaching the child the most common sound-values of the letters.

There is, I think, no need for me in this book to describe the 'phonic word method' materials in detail. Unlike some of the books I have quoted, the *Royal Road Readers* with their explanatory Teacher's Book are readily available. It will be enough to say that the system makes use of pictures and three-letter words arranged in such a way as to teach the child what the letters stand for *in words*. That is to say, the letter 't' is not taught as 'ter' but as the first sound in such words as *top*, *tap*, *tin* and *tub* and the teacher is recommended to amplify the examples by other words within the child's experience, e.g., *tree*, *table*, *tomato*, those irregular words being at the first stages, however, spoken, not written. A further feature of the scheme is that it is so tightly organised that on no page is the child required to interpret a single letter that he has not been taught on one of the previous teaching pages. The common criticism of phonic methods that they ignore *meaning* is met by exercises which the child cannot possibly do without paying attention to the meaning of the sentences he is reading.

The opposition to these ideas continued to show itself in a number of ways. At public lectures this opposition produced very lively discussions among very big audiences. When the Institute of Education at Nottingham advertised a lecture by Daniels and myself, 900 teachers applied for tickets instead of the normal and expected forty to sixty. The discussions that followed the lectures often gave the impression that the meeting had been 'packed' by the 'opposition'. There were no brawls, but arguments frequently spread out into the street and continued long after the meeting had broken up.

Two incidents involving editors of monthly educational journals seemed to me to indicate an unwillingness to publish ideas that were against current opinion. Before *Learning to Read* appeared, the editor of one such journal wrote and asked me to write an article setting forth my ideas about teaching reading in about a thousand words. I did so and then she found that she did not want to publish them after all; we compromised with an article which gave a plain description of the *Royal Road* scheme and from which 'ideas' had been excluded as much as possible. The editor of the struggling *Journal of Education* found himself in a similar position. He also agreed to publish an article but, when he got it, took the unusual step of asking advice about it from the author of a set of reading-books constructed on rather different principles from ours. He then wrote me a letter explaining why the ideas I had expressed in the article were not acceptable to modern educationists. One of his main points was that English spelling was not strictly alphabetic! There was opposition, too, from local advisers to teachers. We heard of a number of instances of advisers making it difficult for teachers to use the *Royal Road Readers* in schools.

For years the argument went on in a great number of papers and journals and it still breaks out now and then.

If one were to judge purely from the published correspondence, one would have the impression that there were two people in Nottingham out of step with the rest of the world and yet in private correspondence there appeared to be a considerable amount of agreement with our ideas. Several local authority psychologists wrote to say how much they agreed with our general point of view. One of them surprised us by commenting on the courage it took to express such views. An Australian educationist, Donald Maclean, wrote a complimentary letter to the *Schoolmaster*. This was in reply to a letter which said that any support we had had for our ideas had come from people outside education and therefore ignorant of what actually went on in schools. To this Maclean replied that he had had the teaching of reading as a main interest for many years, that he had just completed a tour of American educational establishments and had spoken to experts in reading in many parts of the United States and in this country and had come to the conclusion that the teaching materials he had seen in Nottingham were the next logical step in the development of a theory of teaching reading. In his book *What We Want of our Schools*, the American, Irving Adler, wrote in a similar vein.

The views expressed in *Learning to Read* appear very tame now and it is difficult to realise that such a mild expression of opinion should have provoked so many antagonistic outbursts. But they seemed tame also at the beginning of 1955 a year after publication for it was then that there appeared on the American scene a book which set the American educational world by the ears, *Why Johnny Can't Read* by Rudolf Flesch, a book which flayed American reading experts and in doing so stayed in the best-selling lists for thirty-nine weeks.

Flesch wrote his book in the form of a letter to the mother of a child who had found difficulty in learning to read although he was of better than average intelligence. In his view reading meant getting meaning from certain combinations of letters. 'Teach the child what each letter stands for and he can read.'

He attacked the repetitious reading-books that were common in American schools, said that in forsaking the alphabet we had thrown 3,500 years of civilisation out of the window and gone back to the Age of Hammurabi.

If Johnny has brought home one of his books, look at it. You will immediately see that all the words in it are learned by endless repetition. Not a sign anywhere that letters correspond to sounds and that words can be worked out by pronouncing the letters. No. The child is told what each word means and then they are mechanically, brutally hammered into his brain.

This was strong, highly emotive stuff. But that was not all. He attacked the publishing houses who produce books for elementary schools–'by far the most lucrative part of their business'. He gave examples of the repetitious reading material and went on:

Naturally, the stupendous and frighteningly idiotic work of concocting this stuff can only be done by tireless teamwork of many educational drudges. But if the textbook house put only the drudges on the title page, that wouldn't look impressive enough to beat the competition. So there has to be a 'senior author'–someone with a national reputation who teaches how to teach reading at one of the major universities. And that's why each and every one of the so-called authorities in this field is tied up with a series of readers based on the Chinese word-learning method. . . . Consequently it's utterly impossible to find anyone inside the official family of the educators saying anything even slightly favourable to the natural method of teaching reading. Mention the alphabetic method or phonetics or 'phonics' and you immediately arouse derision, furious hostility, or icy silence.

Flesch reported a considerable number of experiments in which pupils taught by a phonic method had proved superior to pupils taught by the accepted word method and added: 'After all this, you possibly expect me now to recite the evidence in favor of the word method. But . . . there is none.'

One of the ideas that came under Flesch's lash was the idea of 'readiness', an idea which he criticised strongly in a chapter called 'Two Years Wasted'. The idea that a six-year-old cannot learn to read, he said, is quite new and a purely American invention. It was not as new as Flesch implied, however, as we have seen from the earlier quotations from Dewey and Patrick. He traced the idea back to an experiment by Dolch and Bloomster reported in the *Elementary School Journal* in November 1937. Those research-workers reached the conclusion that 'phonic readiness' did not develop until a mental age of seven was reached.

I have seen this statement repeated—and explained at length —in every single book on teaching reading that I have studied. The statement is always backed up by scientific evidence. There is always a footnote or bibliographical reference in those books when the subject of 'phonic readiness' is discussed. The footnote is always the same. It refers to one single experimental study in which the onset of phonic readiness at seven was discovered. . . . You'd think it would be rather difficult to prove that six-year-olds can't learn phonics considering the fact that all over the world and through most of recorded history they have done just that.

He then went on to expose the Dolch-Bloomster experiment as unscientific.

Why Johnny Can't Read was to a large extent the expression of a highly personal view of the development of contemporary ideas about teaching reading and since the book I am now writing covers the same ground—and more—in greater detail there is no need for me here to say much more about the actual content of Flesch's book. Unlike some of the other books I have referred to at some length, it is in any case easily available. My purpose in quoting from him has been to give an impression of the tone rather more than of the substance of his book.

From a pre-publication preliminary notice of Flesch's book that I had seen in the American *Bookseller* I had expected to find in Flesch an ally in the attempt to bring what I thought to be commonsense back to the teaching of reading. The book itself was, however, a great disappointment. True, it made good polemical reading, and I was aware that if I had known less about the subject I should have enjoyed the vigour of the writing very much more. It was obvious that a large public would read the book. Indeed it had already begun to do so. The *San Francisco Examiner* had serialised excerpts from it and these had aroused so much interest that the paper had published a special supplement in which teachers, representatives of teachers' organisations, school superintendents, educational administrators and trainers of teachers made strong and usually dignified replies to Flesch's charges.

I began reading Flesch's book already convinced that his general position was right, but I had not read very much of it before I began to see it as not much more than a tissue of the half-truths that those he was attacking had left out of their reckoning. I thought and said that the result of the publication of such a vitriolic attack on current ideas would set back progress by ten years. The ten years are nearly up, but that is the sort of statement of which no amount of time will bring scientific proof. What is certain, however, is that the immediate reaction to *Why Johnny Can't Read* was a closing of the ranks of those who had been so rudely attacked. All over the United States meetings and conferences to discuss the book were held by the hundred. Yards and yards of correspondence appeared in newspapers and magazines. Emeritus Professor Arthur I. Gates, one of those who had been attacked, wrote a pamphlet defending the citadel of orthodox opinion. Meanwhile *Why Johnny Can't Read* continued to pass across the counters at best-selling rates week after week, stirring up anger in the hearts of educationists against the author, impatience and dismay among parents against educationists and filling the members of faculties other than education with malicious glee.

Demolition experts generally knock something down in order that something else may go up in its place. The fact that Flesh had some constructive suggestions was very nearly obscured by the energy and enthusiasm he brought to the demolition work, but he did have some. In fact the second half of his book was given over to what he claimed was a complete scheme for teaching reading. This consisted of a picture alphabet and seventy-two columned pages of words phonically graded, beginning with *mat, jam, rat* and *map* and ending with *liberty, independence, blueberries* and *democracy*. Flesch advised that the child should begin by learning to recognise the letters and associate them with their sounds. Then Johnny was to work through the columns of words, his parent or teacher making sure that he was not at any time guessing at the words. It was to be explained to Johnny that there is a capital as well as a small letter for each sound, but the advice was to concentrate on the small letters first—this, as we shall see, is different from one recent suggestion. The lists of words were to be used to teach writing and spelling as well as reading. This seems to indicate that the names of the letters were to be taught as soon as the decoding of words began. Johnny was not only to say the words but was to write each word from dictation. In the early pages many of the words occur several times; it is not so in the later pages. Nearly a third of the seventy-two pages were review pages. The words were to be taken first from left to right, then horizontally, then vertically. They were also to be read from right to left, from the bottom upwards, diagonally, and by random selection. In the advice to parents and teachers there was no mention of meaning or 'thought-getting'. This omission gave a certain substance to the frequent criticism by Flesch's numerous opponents that he was teaching mere word-calling, but Terman and Walcutt in *Reading : Chaos and Cure* (1958) defend Flesch against this criticism by pointing out that in the text of *Why Johnny Can't Read*, and in other books he had written, Flesch had dealt quite explicitly with the question of meaning in the context of communication. Yet his failure to mention meaning or 'thought-getting' in his suggestions about the reading lessons made it easier for his critics to argue that he had completely rejected the most important contributions to reading theory of 20th-century research.

In 1956, a year before the publication of *Standards of Reading* and a year after the publication of *Why Johnny Can't Read*, the Institute of Education of the University of Nottingham brought out *Progress in Reading* in which J. C. Daniels and I reported the results of an investigation into the value of the letter-based method we had been working on for several years. This method we later named 'the phonic word method' to distinguish it from the various phonic methods that had been tried out in the past. The teaching materials of the phonic word method are embodied in the *Royal Road* series of readers and the investigation reported in *Progress in Reading* compared pupils completely unable to read on entering the junior school who had been taught for a year by means of this material with similar pupils who had been taught for the same length of time by teachers using 'mixed methods' with look-and-say books. Most pieces of educational research produce results that support the investigators' hypotheses and this one was not the exception that proved the rule. The phonic word method pupils were strikingly superior to pupils whose teachers used books designed according to word or sentence method principles. Six tests were given to each group of pupils. Four of these were single-word tests. In doing these tests the pupils were required to read the words aloud. Their responses were recorded on tape and from the tape-recording the errors the children made were analysed.

There is, I think, no need in this book to describe this investigation and its results in detail. At the heart of it were the tests and their results. The four single-word tests were as follows:

Test 1: Twenty words phonically simple selected from the 500 most frequently used words in the English language according to the Thorndike word-count.

Test 2: Twenty words irregularly spelt from the same list of 500 commonest words. Each word in Test 2 was matched with a word in Test 1 as to the number of letters in it.

Test 3: Twenty words selected from Book I of the *Royal Road Readers*. Each word here too was matched with a word in Test 1 according to the number of letters. These words were also regularly spelt since the readers in question were designed as a phonically graded series and the first part of the Book I was designed to test knowledge of the elementary 'meanings' of the letters.

Test 4: Twenty words selected from the first books of word or sentence method reading series. These words were also matched according to length. The actual words of Tests 3 and 4 were these:

Test 3	Test 4
red	her
but	two
cut	you
step	ball
lost	here
bank	ride

Test 3	Test 4
hand	four
help	door
milk	play
black	board
jumps	brush
ponds	horse
plank	laugh
milkman	chimney
given	found
attract	cushion
caravan	another
collected	aeroplane
kennel	little
catapult	curtains

Teachers reading this book may care to see how their pupils score on these tests.

The following table summarises the results of these four single-word tests.

	PUPILS TAUGHT BY PHONICALLY GRADED MATERIAL			PUPILS TAUGHT BY 'MIXED' METHODS		
	Right	Wrong	No response	Right	Wrong	No response
Test 1:	85·5	7·8	6·7	43·1	11·6	45·3
Test 2:	60·5	13·1	26·4	35·2	11·5	53·3
Test 3:	79·9	6·4	13·7	47·7	11·8	40·5
Test 4:	73·5	8·0	18·5	44·9	10·4	44·7
All tests combined:	74·9	8·8	16·3	42·7	11·3	46·0

All the pupils in both groups had at the beginning of

the year failed to record a mark on the word recognition tests used in the schools (Schonell and Ballard). All therefore had progressed throughout the first-year junior school year. Some interesting points emerge from those figures that we did not bring out at the time. It is interesting, for example, that the phonic word method pupils scored more highly on the regularly spelt words from the Thorndike list than from the words selected from the *Royal Road* book. It is interesting, too, that the 'mixed material' pupils' highest score was in the test from the *Royal Road* book, the book they had not been using–an indication that for pupils who can read at all regularly spelt words are easier than irregularly spelt words. The superiority of the phonic word method pupils in the number of correct responses in all four tests is, however, quite striking, though perhaps not more striking than the difference between the 'no response' figures. *In the test of the commonest regularly spelt words there were nearly seven times as many nil responses among the 'mixed material' pupils as there were among the phonic word method pupils*–45·3 *compared with* 6·7. In all four single-word tests combined there were nearly three times as many nil responses among the 'mixed material' pupils as there were among the phonic word method pupils–46·0 compared with 16·3.

Two sentences tests were also given. One set was composed of words from Book I of the *Royal Road Readers* and the other with irregularly spelt words from look-and-say readers. For example, *The man swims from a rock* was matched with *The boy plays with a ball*. These tests did not produce such striking results as the single-word tests. Nor did simple logic expect them to. In allocating marks we merely gave a mark for each word correctly read aloud—for again here the answers were recorded on tape. In tests where context plays a part there is a choice of routes to the answer where the answer is merely reading a word aloud: the word may be suggested by the meaning of other words in the sentence or it may be worked out from a child's knowledge of the letter, or of some of the letters. Nevertheless on these tests the percentage scores of the phonic word method pupils were 87 for the regularly spelt test and 82 for the other, compared with percentages of 62 and 61 for the other group of pupils. These differences were found to be highly significant in statistical terms.

The theory we had worked out was by no means as complicated as the statistical treatment of the test results and the rigorous examination of the children's reading errors in *Progress in Reading* might have made it appear. Indeed I had considerable sympathy with the *Daily Sketch* journalist whose 'review' of the pamphlet amounted to a sentence or two in which he said that after two years' work involving a considerable amount of experiment and the careful application of statistical techniques two lecturers at Nottingham University had reached the conclusion that short words are easier to read than long ones. I should not have found it grossly unfair if he had carried his irony even further and said that after careful examination of printed English, the observation and testing of many children, careful statistical analysis of the children's responses and detailed inspection of the connection between spoken words and print as revealed by children's errors, those two lecturers had reached the conclusion that there are letters in printed English.

It was the length of words he hit upon, however, and I

wonder now whether I was right in assuming that his report was ironical. It might have been a plain statement of fact reported even with some relief. Many parents at the time were extremely puzzled by the presence of long words in early reading-books—so different from the books of some of their schooldays. They really doubted whether it was right that their children should be expected to read words like *breakfast*, *aeroplane* and *ice-cream* before they knew anything about letters. There were several answers to their doubting questions:

It is easier for a child to see the difference between *aeroplane* and *sky* than between *cat* and *mat*. So by beginning with very different shapes you are starting them off in the easiest possible way.

You say short words are easier than long ones. Very well, then, is *ion* easier than *elephant*? Can you say what an *ion* is? And can you explain why far more five-year-olds can read *ice-cream* than can read *with* or *do*?

If you limit the child's reading to short words, you are cutting out of his reading experiences a great number of the words that he has found most interesting—*ice-cream* and so on.

Our theory did indeed mean in practice removing those interesting long words from the child's first reading experiences. We had reached the conclusion that the best way of teaching a child to read is to devise a method that would bring him as quickly and easily as possible to insight and knowledge about letters, what the various letters look like and how they are used. This was by no means a new idea. It was the idea behind most phonic methods, notably *Reading Without Tears* described in an earlier chapter. Yet in the early 1950s a very large number of people found

it very interesting indeed–some had the same kind of
interest in it that a drowning man might have in a straw;
others the sort of interest a china-shop owner displays in a
bull.

In 1958 the attack on unlettered methods of teaching
reading was continued in America by the book I have
already referred to for its defence of Flesch, *Reading :
Chaos and Cure* by Sibyl (*sic*) Terman and C. C. Walcutt.
Physically, this book was not much more substantial than
Why Johnny Can't Read, but on all other counts it was
very much more so. It was very much the book which the
pre-publication notice of Flesch's book had led me to
expect three years earlier. It covered much of the ground
that Flesch had covered, but in a much more scholarly
way. It was as severe in its criticisms of orthodox thought
on the subject but did not have that raw bitterness which
characterised Flesch's writing; it was also more fundamental in its thinking. The authors emphasised particularly two aspects of the matter which had received only
cursory treatment from Flesch: they discussed in some
detail the relationships between the spoken word, the
written word, and meaning, and they paid considerable
attention to the question as to how words are perceived
and the part played by the Gestalt theory of perception in
reading theory.

Their views on the first point are summed up in the
following sentences:

Teaching words as meaningful wholes ignores the basic
fact that *printed words are symbols of sounds* and are made up
of letters which are symbols of sounds. Current theory completely misses the fact that a printed word has meaning *because
it is a symbol of a sound*, a spoken word that already has meaning

for the child. It is not the configuration that means; it is the sound, *which the child already knows*.

In their consideration of Gestalt psychology, Terman and Walcutt came to the conclusion that 'the illogical union' of the Gestalt idea that we see wholes before we see parts with some ill-considered deductions from the study of eye-movements in reading was 'the ultimate theoretical basis of the reading method which today is undermining our educational system'. They quoted a statement from Cronbach's *Educational Psychology* (1954), viz: 'The good reader takes in a whole word or phrase at a single glance, recognising it by its outline.' That statement provided them with a jumping-off point for a brief analysis of word-perception in which they criticised the idea that words are recognised by their outline. The good reader, they said, does not have to look at each letter on the page because the full image of the word is already stored in his brain. This statement, simple though it is, is nevertheless important, and all the more important because it could not have been made by those who accepted the Gestalt theory of perception as it had been interpreted by reading theorists. Flesch, it is true, had given some consideration to Gestalt theory. He had said that the key to Gestalt psychology is the sudden moment of insight, the flash, the click, the psychological experience of having everything fall into place, of suddenly understanding the total structure of a thing. This, he said, is the experience of the child who knows the letters. He argued that if a Gestalt psychologist were asked to work out a system of teaching reading, he would emerge from his laboratory with phonics. He wished the educators were frank about this thing and admitted that

I

the word method is a simple application of the conditioned reflex.

It goes straight back to Pavlov and his famous salivating dogs. . . . It was not long before the conditioned-reflex psychologists . . . found out that Pavlov's discovery can be used to train a human being. . . . Of course you can teach a child to read that way—nothing easier than that. You show him the word *chicken* seventeen times in succession, each time in connection with a picture of a chicken and an explanation by the teacher that this combination of letters means a chicken. . . . Don't you see how degrading the whole process is? The child is never told *why* this heap of letters means 'chicken'. . . . It seems to me a plain fact that the word method consists essentially of treating children as if they were dogs. It is not a method of teaching at all; it is clearly a method of animal training. It's the most inhuman, mean, stupid way of foisting something on a child's mind.

In 1960, J. C. Daniels and I, through the University of Nottingham Institute of Education, published *Progress in Reading in the Infant School*, a report on an investigation in conducting which we had enjoyed the co-operation of a number of infant schools. Two of these schools—one in Bedford and the other in Northants—had been using the *Royal Road Readers*; the others had been using 'mixed methods' with mixed books. By visiting the schools, speaking to the teachers and by putting precise questions about theory and method, we attempted to assess the degree to which phonics appeared in the various mixed methods; we compared the schools according to socio-economic status and tested the children in reading for meaning as well as in word recognition in addition to testing by the Terman-Merrill Revision of the Binet test and by a non-verbal test of the Block Pattern Design variety. In this investigation, too, we failed to find the exception that proves the rule about research in education supporting the hypotheses the research-workers start out with.

In that year, too, I published in Nottingham, and a few months later in New York, *Reading and the Psychology of Perception*. In this book I was largely concerned with Gestalt psychology in relation to reading theory but necessarily had to pay a fair amount of attention to the process of perception itself. One of the main points in the book was that there is a world of difference between the image on the retina and what the brain deduces from the image. This idea was linked with the difference between the learning child and the experienced reader in the perception of words.

Experiment and observation led me to make the following statements about the perception of printed words.

1. Whether a word is previously known in print or not, it is possible to present it for so brief a time that no feature of it is distinguishable; it may appear merely as a grey band or may not be seen at all.

2. If the exposure time is increased, and the subject is given no previous information as to which word to expect, he will see particular details before he sees 'the whole word'.

3. If the subject is led to expect a particular word, he will very frequently see that word in its entirety in as brief a fraction of time as when, without that expectancy, he saw only a detail or two.

4. In certain circumstances a subject will see a printed word in all its details even though all the details are not there. Such circumstances are (a) that he should be

expecting to see that particular word, (b) that what is exposed should bear a fairly close resemblance to what is expected to be seen, (c) that the time of exposure should be brief–how brief depends upon a number of factors, degree of lighting, for example, and degree of familiarity with the printed word.

These experiments and observations demonstrated–quite decisively it seemed to me–that the statements so often made, about children seeing whole words or whole sentences at a glance, were so loose in their meaning as to shiver on the edge of meaninglessness. What precisely was meant by 'see' in such a context? What by 'whole'? All the details or the whole without the details? Most of the errors children made in our *Progress in Reading* investigation could be attributed to a process of seeing part of the printed word quite accurately and saying the whole of another word. Was it not possible that this same part-seeing and whole-saying process went on in the correct reading of words only it was not noticed because no mistake had been made? And yet it often was noticed, though not perhaps thought of in this way, for what else could be taking place when a misprint escaped notice? Suppose a letter had been missed out in the type-setting. There the word complete in all its details could not be seen on the page. Therefore the eye was not 'seeing' the word in all its details. Yet the brain *was*; otherwise the misprint would have been noticed. These observations left me in no doubt whatsoever that in the perception of words a process of visual analysis had to take place. It was not a question, however, of every word having to be visually analysed every time it was seen in print but certainly of every word having to be analysed the first time it was encountered in print, if not oftener. And what about words written by hand. I had friends whose handwriting frequently required a thorough-going visual analysis of even the most familiar words.

In this matter of seeing words complete in every detail even though every detail is not there in the print, inner speech would seem to be intimately involved. The context suggests the word one will 'say' to oneself; the inner saying of the word is the stimulus to the inner seeing of it reinforcing the stimulus that has come from the retina. This seemed a reasonable explanation of one of the more interesting errors in the *Progress in Reading* investigation. The children were required to read *The hens clucked*. One child read 'The hens chickens'. It seems likely that having read and said to himself 'hens' he then said to himself 'chickens'—and finally said them both aloud; it seems likely that he saw the word 'chickens' where a more experienced reader would have seen 'clucked' and that he saw it as clearly as he ever saw that word in his life—and that may not have been very clearly if he had never been asked to look at it carefully. Some of the other errors connected with that particular sentence did not lay themselves so open to that particular explanation: 'The has chimly', 'The hands chicked', 'The hangs kangs', 'The hansh chiskid', and 'The hine clickle'. The last two might be thought to belong to poetry rather than to the skill of reading. Certainly on a summer evening when the air is still I now and then find myself listening into distance for the faint 'clickle' of a 'hine'.

There were, it seemed to me, certain stages in the development of the full perception of printed words which, although merging into one another could nevertheless be regarded as sufficiently distinct not to be purely imaginary categories.

1. In the patterns of light that are reflected into a baby's eyes from the external world there will frequently be print-patterns from various sources—newspapers, cereal packets, neon signs. They are in the eye, as one might say, but not necessarily seen, for obviously we never 'see' more than a fraction of what at any moment lies within the physical limits of perception in one eye-fixation. Rarely, perhaps, a young baby may be conscious of that part of the retinal image which the adult knows to be print—as when the letters of a neon-sign flash brightly enough to catch the attention. But there can be no possible realisation of that light as print.

2. There is a stage when he is likely to pay attention and even ask questions about print, as when he sees marks on a wall and says, 'What's that?'

3. There is a stage where he begins, perhaps because of his previous questioning, to associate some of the print with meaning, as when he may learn to distinguish the packet containing one kind of cereal from another, the print as well as the colour of pictures being part of the set of details through which he distinguishes that particular packet from others.

4. There is a stage at which the child learns to associate print with meaning. It may occasionally, because of particular circumstances, be the 'general shape' that he associates with meaning but more often he seizes upon details. He will be content with any detail that serves his purpose and that purpose is usually to enjoy the recognition of something familiar and the praise which this achievement brings from his parents. Very often at this

stage the child will recognise in this inaccurately perceived way so many words as to give the impression that he can read.

5. There is a stage where he begins to associate particular parts of printed words with the sound-parts of spoken words. The irregular spelling of English makes it unlikely that this association will take place without guidance of a special character. For the child to discover the relationship for himself in a regularly spelt language would denote exceptional powers of reasoning. Yet this is the important stage in learning to read. A vocabulary that is regularly spelt has the great advantage of giving the child confidence in his ability to work things out for himself. Also because there is a constant relationship between the visual appearance of the letter and the sound it represents there will be reciprocity between the senses of sight and sound. The child will see the printed word more accurately and hear and speak his mother tongue more accurately.

6. There is the stage which all readers of this book have reached, the stage at which they are so familiar with printed words that they seldom have to pay conscious attention to the letters. They can read a whole book without seeing more than a part of it in the ordinary sense of the word *see*. They tell themselves from the context what they are going to see and therefore see it. (I had pointed out earlier in the book that the simple word 'see' is one of the most difficult words in the language because of the complexities that lie behind it.)

These then were the stages of progress towards full reading ability that I described in *Reading and the Psychology of Perception*. I pointed out at the same time that the reader at stage 6 may at any time have to revert to stage 5, to letter-by-letter examination of a word because it is completely new to him.

In America, as correspondence and the arrival of travelling investigators showed, the campaign for more attention to letters continued. A body called the Council for Basic Education was very active in this field, and still is. It is not regarded with great favour by most of the professional educationists. In 1961 this body published a volume called *Tomorrow's Illiterates*. In this book J. C. Daniels and I collaborated with the editor, Charles C. Walcutt, joint author of *Reading: Chaos and Cure*, to the extent of contributing a chapter called 'The Nature of Reading Skill'. Also in collaboration with him we published as a paper-back in the Cornerstone Library *Your Child and his Reading* (1964), a guide to parents, and so the commerce of ideas across the Atlantic, which was so notable a feature in earlier days, continues in this.

Another recently established body in the United States is the Reading Reform Foundation, more specialised in its interests than the Council for Basic Education but no less active.

Chapter Seven

LINGUISTICS AND READING

THE title of this chapter is also the title of one of the most recent books about reading, written by C. C. Fries, a professor of linguistics at the University of Michigan, and published in 1963. The chapter is not, however, a review of that book, but an indication that enough of 20th-century thinking about reading has come from the field of linguistics to justify a separate treatment, chapter-length, of this topic. It is only in recent years that the specialist periodicals have been carrying articles with such titles as 'The Linguistic Approach to Reading' and 'What has Linguistics to tell us about Reading?' And yet it is not quite accurate to claim as a wholly 20th-century development the idea that there is a connection between linguistics and reading. What may indeed be a fair statement is that the high-level study of language has broadened out so greatly from the study of comparative philology which it so largely was in the 19th century that even the problems of teaching little children to read are now within the scope of linguistics or in the margins of it.

The latter half of the 19th century and the first half of the 20th saw the development of new language disciplines – the genetic or developmental study of language in the individual, semantics that concerned itself not only with shifts of meaning but with the nature of meaning itself, communication theory which both led to and developed out of the highly complicated instruments of the modern telecommunicative world. And yet of course there is an element of linguistic thinking behind every reading method. Anybody who thinks about the teaching of reading at all has to think in some sort of fashion about the relationship between visual signs, spoken language, meaning and the communication of meaning. Some of the thinking was indeed very elementary and had hardly the shadow of a connection with scientific linguistics. Then again, in the days when comparative philology was the major language study, the teaching of reading fell, for other reasons than its apparently elementary nature, well outside the province or interest of those men who sat in professorial chairs that would nowadays be called chairs of linguistics.

In recent years at least three linguistic specialists have entered the arena in which the battle of the alphabet is being fought—L. Bloomfield, C. L. Barnhart and C. C. Fries. I might have included in this section the names of a number of people from the 16th century onwards who have advocated, in the interest of easy reading, some modification of English spelling because that is essentially a linguistic matter, but the idea of using a special orthography for the teaching of reading is discussed in a later chapter and so of the pre-20th-century writers on reading I include only Sonnenschein in this section.

It would have been quite reasonable to include Sonnenschein in the chapter on phonic methods and that was my first intention but as I became better acquainted with his ideas it seemed to me that he was essentially a 'language' man; he was not involved like Nellie Dale with the children; he was involved rather with the written structure of the language they were learning to read. He was in

fact very much akin to Bloomfield and Fries although his
method and materials were different. Sonnenschein's first
publication that had to do with reading was published in
collaboration with a Professor Meiklejohn in 1869. It
was called *The English Method of Teaching to Read*. Later,
towards the end of the century he published a set of three
little books for teaching children to read with the title
Reading in a Twelve-month and with them a 'Teacher's
Companion'. His books were very popular in England
during the last decade or so of the 19th century and the
first of the 20th.

The very title of *The English Method of Teaching to
Read* gives an indication of Sonnenschein's approach. He
believed that the method and materials suitable for teaching children to read vary from one language to another
even though all the languages concerned are written down
by means of the same alphabet; the differences will arise
from the way in which the alphabet is used. He thought,
for example, that reading in Italian and German would be
most effectively taught by means of what he called the
'literal' or 'reading by spelling' method—that is, one of the
alphabetic methods. His reason for thinking so was that
both these languages had a largely phonetic spelling. In
both English and French, however, 'where simple sounds
are often represented by groups of letters, the true elements
of words as far as spelling is concerned are syllables, and
the syllabic (i.e., according to Sonnenschein, the phonic)
method is indispensable'. It is interesting here to note the
diametric contrast between Sonnenschein's view and that
of the later word method advocates who maintained that
the irregularity of English spelling was the very reason
why a phonic method was not applicable to the language

whereas it might well be the most suitable for languages that were more regular in their spelling.

In the chapter on word methods I quoted Sonnenschein's classification of the various methods of teaching reading and pointed out that in equating syllabic and phonic methods he was not exactly clarifying matters for anybody who was trying to understand the evolution of ideas about the teaching of reading. Yet his own method and ideas were clear enough to himself and in his *Teacher's Companion* he made them clear enough to other people. He quotes with approval the statement of Bain, the logician and philosopher, in his book *Education as a Science*: 'The preferable plan seems to be to carry the pupils forward on perfectly uniform spellings so that they may get the idea of regularity and all the most prevalent sounds of the letters.' Bain had emphasised the difference between teaching an ideographically written language, like Chinese, and an alphabetically written language and had said that the only way of reducing the 'Chinese operation to its narrowest limit' was to make full use of the principle of minimising exceptions. Until somebody had gone through 'the labour (not small) of classifying the existing spellings under uniformities and exceptions', learning to read, in his view, would not be made as easy as it might be. Sonnenschein seems to have quoted Bain chiefly for the pleasure of showing that 'the learned professor' had not realised that the not small labour had already been completed and the results of the labour published 'by the author in his book entitled *The English Method of Teaching to Read*'—no mention here of Meiklejohn his collaborator. On the same line of thought, of course, Sonnenschein ought himself to have known that in the previous century

Webster in America, working on a related principle, had gone through the labour of classifying English spelling with the same end in view which was, in Sonnenschein's words, 'to present to the learned in systematic and graduated sequence all the phenomena of English reading and spelling'.

The first section in Sonnenschein's teaching scheme taught the pupils by a look-and-say method all the two-letter words in the English language. He found forty-three of these which seems a fair achievement in itself. These two-letter words were taught in groups systematically 'so that the words aid and illustrate each other'. And here we may note how different a form of look-and-say this is from the look-and-say of the 'configuration method' where differences in the lengths of the words was regarded as an important factor.

The next section taught 'the force' of the five short vowels with plenty of drill and with a blackboard scheme set out as follows:

    at: bat – fat – hat –   mat – pat – rat – sat
    it: bit – fit – hit – lit –   pit –   sit.

and so on with *et*, *ot* and *ut*. The omission of *cat* from the first line is due to the fact that the hard and soft sounds of the letter *c* are taught together at a later stage. There is no need for me to go through Sonnenschein's grading in detail, but one or two further points need to be made.

One of the leading maxims of good teaching, he says, is that *telling is not teaching*. For this reason, he argues, the look-and-say method should be very sparingly used: 'It is mere telling, mere appeal to the memory, the lowest of our mental faculties, and no exercise of the learner's intelligence.' His view is that as in every other subject of study, the child must, as far as possible, be led to the discovery of the fact by his own logical or analogical reasoning.

He goes on:

The whole art of reading consists of the knowledge and instant recognition of certain arbitrary symbols representing sounds; these the pupil must be *told*, but all subsequent interpretation of symbols should be derived from the knowledge thus imparted. If the child stops at a new or a long word, the components of which have already been taught, then he should not be told the word, but should be led to build it up on the blackboard in some such manner as the following:

PENMANSHIP: en, pen; an, man; penman; ip, ship; penmanship.

The final point I have to make about Sonnenschein is that he worked according to the formula that the apparent anomaly ceases to be one if it can be proved to be the expression of a law. He says that we must guard ourselves against the exaggerations of spelling reformers who have argued that the irregularities of English spelling are so great a burden. No doubt, he said, if the spelling reformers had their way the problem of teaching reading would be a much lighter one, but so far the language had to be dealt with as it is.

We come now to Leonard Bloomfield's theory of teaching reading. Bloomfield, who died in 1949 while still a professor of linguistics at Yale, was a major figure in the field of linguistics in the years between the wars, and his book *Language*, published in 1933, is still regarded as a classic in that sector of organised knowledge. He was not only a linguist, he was also a father, and like many other parents, including Sonnenschein, he taught his son

to read. Some parents teach their children to read because
they want their offspring to get off to a good start schol-
astically; some because they feel that even amateur individual attention is better than the insufficient professional
attention that is possible in large classes; some because
they think the way they themselves were taught to read is
the best. Bloomfield taught his son to read because he had
reached the conclusion that the methods used in the schools
were non-scientific in nature and ignored the fundamental
principles of language developed during the previous
century and a half. In order to teach his son, he devised
teaching materials which he believed were in keeping
with these fundamental principles. Between 1937 and the
year of his death these teaching materials were offered for
trial and experiment to the schools of education at three
large universities noted for their experimental work in
education, to various state school systems, and to publishers of educational books. After Bloomfield's death,
Barnhart, with whom he had formed a partnership to try
to market the Bloomfield system, continued to try to
interest educationists and publishers in the material with
a total lack of success. The material was not thought to be
a viable commercial proposition. However, in 1958, one
of the charitable foundations in which America is not
lacking made Barnhart a grant to prepare the Bloomfield
materials for publication and see them through the press
and so in 1961 there appeared under the aegis of Wayne
University *Let's Read: A Linguistic Approach*, a substantial quarto volume of 465 pages at a price of seven and
a half dollars and containing the Bloomfield teaching
material with additions by Barnhart and essays by various
hands including Bloomfield's, but no pictures except for

some line-drawings on three pages as part of a pre-reading test. Barnhart emphasises that this is an experimental edition worked out and designed for widespread experiment in the United States. 'The most useful experiment,' he writes, 'would be one in which the Bloomfield system was used exclusively in teaching reading whether in a church kindergarten or in a public school kindergarten or in a first grade. It would be helpful if a statistician and a linguist assisted educators in formal experiment.'

Bloomfield set out his ideas about reading in an essay which Barnhart includes in *Let's Read*. This essay 'Teaching Children to Read' was not to my knowledge ever published in full before but most of it appeared in two separate articles in successive issues of the *Elementary English Review* in the spring of 1942. It reached a wider public still and was kept for a longer period before the attention of educators generally by W. S. Gray who in the *first* edition of his *On Their Own in Reading* gave a very full and fair impression of Bloomfield's articles by summary and copious extracts.

There are, I think, two main reasons why Bloomfield's ideas did not make very much of an impact. The first is that he wrote too simply and he was writing at a time when the educational world was remarkably invulnerable to direct and simple statements though apparently vulnerable to polysyllables. That was an aspect of linguistics that Bloomfield had perhaps neglected. The second is that he was too relentless in his divorce of the *skill* in reading from the *art* of reading and produced as a result teaching materials that were too far removed from the 'thought-getting' and 'interest' pattern that had developed during the previous three or four decades. Indeed his teaching

materials were so like some of the phonic materials of the
19th century that it is quite certain that the educationists
who saw his material were immediately set against his
ideas. In the spread of educational ideas the sheer bulk
of the writing plays a great part. A nexus of ideas that
could be expressed on the back of an envelope carries
much less weight than the same ideas spread out into a
500-page book. Bloomfield's 24 pages of quarto stood little
chance against the great tomes that were pouring from the
presses, but even so it is doubtful whether he could
have by any amount of writing overcome the handicap
of the teaching materials his theory produced.

In his essay Bloomfield asserted that in the teaching
of reading as it was being carried on there was a great
waste of time and labour. This was not due to a lack of
pedagogical techniques but to the simple fact that teachers
did not know what to teach. If teachers did not know *what*
to teach, the most efficient techniques would not be of
very much avail. The waste of time and labour would
go on until teachers of young children became aware
of the linguistic facts and principles that play a part
in the act of reading. So he went on to set out–'in a
practically useful arrangement'–these necessary facts and
principles.

The first of his principles concerns the relationship
between written (or printed) words and speech and his
point here is that language consists of sounds made by
the speaker's vocal organs and that writing is a matter of
recording these sounds. All the various systems of writing
consist of three devices or various mixtures of the three–
picture-writing, which was highly developed by some
American Indian tribes; word-writing of which the best

K

example is Chinese and which we have in our numerals, and alphabetic writing.

Bloomfield defines alphabetic writing as a system in which each character represents a *unit speech sound* and points out that the existence of unit speech sounds, technically called *phonemes*, is one of the discoveries of the study of language in the past hundred years. He illustrates the alphabetic principle by means of a number of three-letter words, e.g., *pin*, *pig*, *pit*, *nip*, but goes on to say that the nature of alphabetic writing appears most plainly of all when we put together a combination of letters that does not make a word and yet find ourselves guided to the utterance of English speech sounds as with *nin*, *mip*, and *lib*. He points out that the reversal of the order of letters in *pin* produces a different word, *nip*, but I am surprised that he does not make this point fully articulate by stating quite precisely that the order of the letters as they appear on the page—in English from left to right—represents the order in time of the spoken sounds; space used to represent time.

In order to read alphabetic writing, Bloomfield goes on, one must have an ingrained habit of producing the phonemes of one's language at the sight of the visual signs that have been devised to represent those phonemes. 'It is this habit which we must set up in the child who is to acquire the art of reading. If we pursue any other course, we are merely delaying him until he acquires this habit in spite of our bad guidance.'

He next has a short section on irregularities of spelling reaching a very different conclusion from Jagger's who emphasised the non-alphabetic, what he exaggeratedly called the 'ideographic', nature of English spelling. For

Bloomfield 'in its basic character, in its bones, blood, and marrow, our system of writing is alphabetic—witness merely the fact that we get along with twenty-six characters instead of twenty-six thousand.'

These comments on spelling are followed by a critical discussion of phonic methods, 'the word method' and 'ideational' methods.

He finds fault with phonic methods on two grounds: (1) the inventors of phonic methods confuse writing with speech and plan the work as though the children were being taught to speak, giving advice about phonetics, about clear utterance and so on, all of which confuses the issue; (2) phonic methods isolate the speech sounds; children are shown, say, the letter *t* and are required to produce that sound in isolation, but this phoneme does not occur in isolation in spoken English; by insisting that the child perform unaccustomed feats with his vocal organs we confuse his response to the printed signs.

Word methods, however, present the most serious drawback in the teaching of reading. Bloomfield's reason for making this statement is that word methods conceal the alphabetic principle from the child. The irregularities of English demand careful handling if they are not to confuse the child and delay his acquisition of the alphabetic habit and so a grading according to the degree of irregularity is necessary, regular spellings being presented in the early stages.

The weakness of ideational methods, the chief of which is the sentence method, is that they expect the child to read in an adult manner. The highly practised adult has so reduced the speech element in reading that he may seem to get the 'ideas' direct from the printed page and expects the child to do the same—'to jump directly from an illiterate state to that of an overtrained reader'.

The letters in a piece of English writing do not represent *things* or, if you prefer, *ideas*. The task of the reader is to get the *sounds* from the written or printed page. When he has done this, he must still of course, perform a second task: he must understand the meaning of these sounds. This second task, however, is not peculiar to reading, but concerns all use of language; when we are not reading, but hearing spoken words, we have the same task of appreciating the content of what is said. The ideational methods, in short, show us the age-old confusion between the use of writing and the ordinary processes of speech.

Now what is Bloomfield's own answer? First the child should be made acquainted with the letters. They have queer and interesting shapes and are made more interesting if printed in colour. One should begin with the capital letters and then go on to the small ones. The child should be familiar with all the letters before reading is begun because we do not want the reading of words to be upset at any stage by the appearance of unfamiliar shapes.

The actual reading lessons begin as follows. The word

can

is shown to the child. The child already knows the names of the letters and is asked to name the letters in their order: *see, ay, en*. The parent or teacher then says: 'Now we have spelled the word. Now we are going to *read* it. This word is *can*. Read it: *can*.' Next the parent or teacher shows another word with the same vowel and final consonant, but with a different initial, e.g., *fan* and goes through the same procedure. This is followed by practice until the child can say the right word of these two whether presently singly or both together.

This may be the complete first lesson of the actual reading scheme, i.e. after the learning of the letter-shapes and -names. But eventually and with increasing speed the child works through the first page of the teaching material which is as follows:

can Dan fan man Nan pan ran tan an ban van

a can   a fan   a pan   ran   a man   a van

a tan van   a tan fan

Dan ran.   Nan ran.

Van ran.   A man ran.

Nan can fan Dan.

Can Dan fan Nan?

Dan can fan Nan.

Nan, fan Dan.

Dan, fan Nan.

Dan ran a van.

Dan ran a tan van.

A man ran a tan van.

From the combination *an*, the teaching material goes on to similar permutations with *at*, *ad*, *ap*, *ag*, *am*, *ab*, *al*, and then to similar exercises with the short 'i' and so on. All this was far too much like the phonic material of the 19th century that had been so much ridiculed that there was not the slightest chance of its being welcomed by educators or educational publishers. 'Can a pig jig in a wig?' asked a 19th-century reading-book compiler. 'Can a big, fat pig jig?' asked Bloomfield on his *ig* page after he had asserted that Sal had a big pig, that Pam had a big fig and that Nan had a wig. No amount of asserting that this scheme was linguistically based or that the words were not being broken up into artificial sound-units could carry that material through the barriers of the modern psychological approach.

C. C. Fries in *Linguistics and Reading* says that the few comments made on Bloomfield's essay show that it has not been understood. He gives as evidence of this misunderstanding Rudolf Flesch's use of Bloomfield's essay to support his 'back to phonics' campaign, Anderson and Dearborn's use of it to support a word method, and W. S. Gray's ignoring of the fact that Bloomfield's method always uses 'whole words', never separated or isolated sounds of letters. Fries's criticism of Gray is based on this sentence from this writer's *On Their Own in Reading*: 'One recent proposal for a mechanical approach to reading denounces any learning of words as wholes in the early stages—and proposes instead use of the alphabetic principle.' He takes the sentence right out of context and as it stands it sounds like nonsense, for how would one make use of the alphabetic principle without drawing attention to the letters and how could one do that while always learning words as wholes? Both Fries and Gray are here, of course, dispensing half-truths. The history of ideas about reading is, however, packed with such ambivalent statements. In writing this book I have very often had to resist strong temptations to indulge myself in niggling at some of the more irritating ones. I make an exception in this case because, when Gray's half-truth is added—by what algebra?—to Fries's, a revealing whole truth emerges and it is that 'words as wholes' may be thought of in terms of speech or of the visual signs of speech. Bloomfield certainly did not begin with words as *seen* wholes because he made sure that first of all the children could identify all the letters singly; but when the actual reading of words was reached he did insist on words as *spoken* wholes. Compare this with the part-seeing and whole-saying detected among children's errors in *Progress in Reading*.

Fries became interested in the teaching of reading as a result of discussion with Bloomfield in the 1930s and his book, *Linguistics and Reading*, can be described as a greatly expanded version of Bloomfield's essay together with Fries's original emphasis and a different solution to the problem. Bloomfield said in a sentence that he found current methods of teaching reading unscientific; Fries traces the origins of those unsatisfying theories quoting at length from the writers responsible for them. Bloomfield states simply and briefly that current reading theory ignores the scientific work on language of the past century and a half; Fries expounds very carefully and in non-technical language what that work was and gives its results. In fact he sets down what he thinks is the minimum a teacher of reading ought to know about linguistics.

All this is extremely interesting if for no other reason than that Fries says things about reading that are not elsewhere to be found in the vast literature on the subject. This literature is indeed so vast that it would take the special abilities of a Saintsbury or a Sidney Webb to become acquainted with all of it. For people less well endowed one thing alone makes a reasonable coverage possible and it is that out of any twenty books on the subject only one will be found to say anything significantly different from the rest. Fries's is one of the different ones.

Unfortunately it is also one of those books where the travelling is very much better than the arriving. Unfortunately, too, for English readers he will appear to look on the past and present of reading through a rather narrow window overlooking Main Street. Reading this book, one would never guess that pupils are being taught to read English in Britain and the Commonwealth as well as in Kalamazoo and Peoria.

Well, then, what has Fries to say? A great deal of it, it seems to me, is plain commonsense. His basic concept of what reading is cannot be gainsaid. Here it is:

Learning to read in one's native language is learning to shift, to transfer, from auditory signs for the language signals, which the child has already learnt, to visual or graphic signs for the same signals. Both reading and talking have the same set of language signals for language *reception*. In talking, contrastive bundles of sound features represent these signals; in reading, contrastive patterns of spelling represent these same signals.

There is perhaps a trace of jargon in that statement, but the meaning comes through. From that basic concept there follows Fries's stated aim in the teaching of reading; it is to develop high-speed recognition responses to English spelling-patterns—to teach the child to take in through the eye the same meanings that, in learning to speak, he learned to take in through the ear.

How does he propose to do this? First of all the child must develop 'recognition responses' to the letters of the alphabet. The goal here is high-speed identification with 100 per cent. accuracy because insufficient mastery of this first step, it is claimed, will inevitably cause confusion and delay later. For the first steps only capital letters—unadorned, i.e. sans serif capitals—should be used in contrast to Bloomfield who began with the lower-case letters. The letters are not taught in alphabetical order, nor is it necessary that the child should have learned to recognise all the letters before he begins to recognise words, but he should not be required to recognise words containing letters he has not been taught to identify. The order he suggests as being the order that has proved most free from confusions is:

1. the stroke letters:

```
I   T   L   F   E   H
A   N   M   K   Z
V   W   X   Y
```

2. the letters combining 'strokes' and 'parts of circles'

```
D   B   P   R
U   J
```

3. the 'circle' letters:

```
O   Q   G   C
S
```

There follows a large amount of practice in the sheer recognition of letter-patterns, at this stage always in sanserif capitals. So we get columns of letter-combinations rather like visual discrimination tests, as:

(A)		(B)		(C)	
I	T	IF	IT	FIT	TIF
T	T	TF	TF	FIF	FIE

The pupil's task is purely and simply to say whether the items in the pairs are the same or different. The intention is to develop 'automatic habits of recognition for the letter-shapes'. Fries emphasises that there should be no attempt to connect the letters themselves with sounds. Nor should any of the combinations that happen to spell words be shown to be words or be pronounced.

In Fries's view it misleads the pupil to seek constantly to match each of the individual letters of which a word is made up with the sounds that make up its pronunciation. 'The assumption that learning to read is learning to match words, as written, letter by letter, with words, as pronounced, sound by sound, constitutes the basic difficulty with *phonics* as a method of teaching reading.' At this point we come to the real core of Fries's method:

Instead of the approach through trying to match the individual letters and separate sound units, we must develop the automatic habits of responding to the contrastive features *of spelling-patterns as identifying the word-patterns they represent.* For example, even in the three letter word, *man*, it is not the single letter *A* that indicates the vowel sound. It is the spelling-pattern *man* in contrast with the spelling-pattern *mane* or that of *mean* that signals the different vowel phonemes that make these three different words. Each of these three is one of the major regular spelling-patterns of English.

Fries, then, suggests a graduated course in the automatic recognition of spelling-patterns. The progression of the materials is to be 'programmed' so that each new item is tied by a simple contrast to an item previously practised. He gives an example of such a progression. Note that there is no breaking up of the words either into letters, visually, for the child has had a great deal of practice in spelling-pattern recognition, or into separate sounds. The teacher pronounces the words 'in talking fashion'.

```
AT – CAT              CAT – RAT
A CAT – A RAT         AT – CAT – RAT – PAT
PAT A CAT            PAT A RAT
        RAT – PAT – FAT
 A FAT CAT              A FAT RAT
 PAT A FAT CAT          PAT A FAT RAT
```

and so on till we reach

```
       A CAT BATS AT A RAT
       CATS BAT AT RATS
```

Fries states that even from the beginning there must be complete meaning responses, 'including the spontaneous social-cultural responses of realising the near-absurdity or humour of a situation with "a cat at bat"'. Like Bloomfield, however, he is stretching optimism to the limit if he expects a scheme of teaching that has so much of the early 19th century about it to be accepted in a world where the reading material for children is expected to be meaningful and interesting.

Chapter Eight

THE INITIAL TEACHING ALPHABET

VARIOUS attempts have been made to solve some of the problems of teaching reading by changing the appearance of orthodox print, e.g., by the use of colour, diacritical marks, or changes in spelling. Sir James Pitman's Initial Teaching Alphabet is a modern instance of this type of teaching aid. This alphabet, known as i.t.a., was developed from the Phonotypy of Isaac Pitman which was tried out in America in the 19th century. In devising the initial teaching alphabet, Sir James also had in mind some of the features of the Nue Speling of the Simplified Spelling Society of Great Britain.

The initial teaching alphabet when it was first introduced to the public a few years ago was known as the Augmented Roman Alphabet. The new name was brought in to remove some misunderstandings or failures in understanding caused by the old name; there was little change in the actual alphabet itself. It is now the habit of those who are involved with the initial teaching alphabet to refer to it as i.t.a.–there are no special forms for capital letters, only majuscules, or lower-case letters writ large. Traditional orthography similarly is referred to as t.o. The type faces for i.t.a. were designed by Sir James Pitman in association with executives of the Monotype Corporation. The outcome of the collaboration was highly ingenious. See facing page.

It will be noted that only q and x of the letters in the

THE INITIAL TEACHING ALPHABET

a	ɑ	æ	au	b
apple	arm	angel	author	bed

c	ch	d	ee	e
cat	chair	doll	eel	egg

f	g	h	ie	i
finger	girl	hat	tie	ink

j	k	l	m	n
jam	kitten	lion	man	nest

ŋ	œ	o	ω	ꭳ
king	toe	on	book	food

ou	oi	p	r	ɼ
out	oil	pig	red	bird

s	ſh	ʒ	t	th
soap	ship	treasure	tree	three

th	ue	u	v	w
mother	due	up	van	window

wh	y	z	ʒ
wheel	yellow	zoo	is

Printers use the 'ɑ' in words like path where regional pronunciation differs. Teachers and children use a or ɑ, whichever
corresponds to their own speech.

present alphabet are not used. Rational spelling systems usually reject the letter *c* as well. In i.t.a. *c* is retained even though it duplicates the work of *k*. The reason for this retention is that it reduces the number of changes in the general shapes, or outline shapes of words–'cat' does not have to be changed to 'kat'.

In order to make the transition from i.t.a. to orthodox as easy as possible, the new letters were designed to have as great a similarity as possible to those they replaced. The designers have been so successful in this that few people find a page of i.t.a. more difficult to read at first sight than a page of moderately legible handwriting. The 'word-patterns' are not greatly altered, largely because the main changes are in the lower halves–it is the top halves of the letters which are the distinctive parts.

At this time of writing, there is being conducted what the Director of the University of London Institute of Education describes as 'one of the most interesting, difficult, and potential pieces of experimental research work the London Institute of Education has ever undertaken'. The investigation is designed 'to discover whether children can learn to read more easily through the augmented version of our present alphabet before they transfer to the normal one'. The National Foundation for Educational Research is collaborating in the investigation. The Government has publicly expressed its belief in the importance of the project and certain sums of money from both public and private sources have been made available for the prosecution and continuance of the research. Yet not many years ago anyone who proposed tampering with the spelling of English was regarded as 'a bit of a crank'. Now the situation has changed to such an extent that any teacher who is not familiar with what i.t.a. means is hardly 'with' it. How did this change come about?

The change is due chiefly to the indefatigable labours of Sir James Pitman himself who has for a long time—and in the family tradition—been intensely interested both in a simplified form of spelling and in the teaching of reading. In the House of Commons, in the Press, and on public platforms, not only in this country, he has over a period of years urged with great cogency the case for a rationalisation of English spelling.

For a number of years Sir James (then Mr. I. J. Pitman) was in close collaboration with the late Mr. M. Follick, whose primary interest was not in the teaching of reading but in the rationalisation of English spelling and who in 1949 introduced into Parliament a Simplified Spelling Bill which aimed at the abolition of irregularities in English spelling in one fell swoop. That Bill met with a fate it may not have deserved. But three years later, on 19th November, 1952, Mr. Follick as a private member introduced another Simplified Spelling Bill, this time with a significant difference. The intention now was not to rationalise English spelling but 'to make provision for the determination of a suitable system of simplified spelling and for the investigation of the improvements in the reading ability of children likely to result from the introduction of this system and to facilitate the subsequent introduction of the system in certain schools'. (*Journal of the House of Commons.*)

It will be noted that the investigation was not to be into whether or not the reading abilities of the children concerned would improve, but into the improvements which it was assumed were likely to occur. The use of the term 'simplified' in the title of the Bill does, of course, make the assumption that it is easier to learn to read in a regularly spelt language than in an irregularly spelt one, and a very large number of people accept that assumption. But that was not the assumption behind the Bill. The question to be investigated was not how much more easily children could learn to read English in a simplified spelling, but how much better they were at reading English in orthodox print as a result of being taught to read English printed in the simplified spelling that had been deemed suitable after investigation.

The Bill was debated in February 1953. Mr. Pitman opened the debate by stating that some 400,000 to 500,000 five-year-olds began their schooling every year, and some 120,000 to 150,000 were destined to come out of the school system at the other end unable to read properly. Questioned as to the basis of that statement he replied, 'The Ministry of Education Pamphlet'—meaning *Reading Abilities*, 1947.

He displayed the word 'telephone' in two forms:

TELEPHONE   telephone

and brought members' attention to the fact that except for the *p* and the *o* there was no resemblance between the two forms of any of the letters. He then went on to point out that another form is used in handwriting: 'The writing forms of all Honourable Members of the House are in fact 625 different word-forms and yet thanks to contexts and thanks to our reading ability we can do these transitions to almost anybody's handwriting.'

Mr. Pitman then went on to discuss the nature of alphabetic writing. The argument is a familiar and, I think, impeccable one. An alphabet is a system of signs that stand for the sounds of speech. The fact that our system of spelling so often departs from the principle of alphabetic writing is a very real stumbling block for both teacher and pupil in the learning and teaching of reading.

Mr. Gordon Walker supported the Bill on terms that could hardly have had Mr. Pitman's full approval. He wanted to restore flexibility and liberty to the spelling of our language: 'I regard it,' he said, 'as a great denial of a man's liberty to compel him to spell in a false and artificial way. . . . There was a time when Englishmen would not have stood for this artificial dragooning of their right to spell as they wished.' He went on to blame Dr. Johnson as the chief criminal in this case. Dr. Johnson received an additional share of blame from another member. On the whole, however, the Bill had an easy passage. One or two members thought that it would be more to the point to reduce the size of the classes; another said that in his opinion there were already too many cranky ideas being tried out in schools by psychologists—not that the men behind the Bill were cranks, nor that the ideas in the Bill were cranky, but that was the situation in the schools. It would be more to the point to let teachers get on with their job in the normal way. Another member thought that things were being made too easy for children anyway. An interesting contribution to the debate came from Dr. A. D. D. Broughton who congratulated Mr. Follick on his manner of drafting an apparently innocent Bill, but the debate as it had so far proceeded had revealed beneath an innocent surface a design with which he could not agree. 'I regard the Bill,' he said, 'as the thin edge of

L

a wedge, later to be driven in, for radical change in the spelling of the English language.'

It was natural that such a suspicion should have stirred in the minds of some members because of what they recalled of Mr. Follick's previous effort. The editor of the *Times Educational Supplement* in his editorial at the time showed in a guarded way that the idea that the new Bill was part of a tactic working towards a general reform of English spelling had crossed his mind too.

Mr. Pitman had taken steps to inform teachers what lay behind the Bill. In a front page article in the *Teacher's World* he had explained that his concern was about the level of reading ability, and the fact that he was not satisfied with the state of literacy in England did not amount to an attack upon teachers. He then went on to give his reasons for claiming that the transfer from reading English in a simplified spelling to reading English in orthodox spelling would be quick. There were three such reasons:

1. More than half of the words on any one page will remain unchanged and even in the rest the degree of alteration will be such as to furnish a clue from which the solution will often 'jump' to the eye.

2. The value of context is very great when the eye can travel quickly both forward and *backward* over the sentence *as a whole*. Even WUN of these words which—and they are very rare—are so little related to the other form that a blank would be equally helpful, is readily guessed by the fluent reader—even when it is spelled ONE.

3. The child already makes a few more difficult transitions from BAD to 'bad' and then to bad (written)—which as *The Times* has pointed out is equivalent to learning the Greek alphabet and then adding literacy in the Arabic and Cyrillic forms.

Mr. Pitman went on to give his reasons for expecting with confidence better reading progress, faster and more surely, if the alphabet were used alphabetically. These were:

1. Young children when left to themselves write alphabetically and it is always easier to learn that which comes naturally.

2. Look-and-say is an end-objective, not a means. If it were a means, modern Chinese script and the pre-alphabetic picture-writing would be as easy to learn as alphabetic script and they are not because.

(a) The 5001st word to a Chinese student is no easier than the first.

(b) The Chinese student requires the teacher's aid over every word.

Authoritarian didacticism is the *only* method in such a script. The student is unable to fall back upon himself to solve his difficulties or to overcome his hesitancies.

In *The Schoolmaster*, too, as the official N.U.T. journal was at that time called, Mr. Pitman explained the nature of the purpose of the Bill in a letter to which a teacher M.P. Mr. Ralph Morley, was co-signatory. In the light of later events it is interesting to note that this letter pointed out that the Bill provided 'that other experiments to be decided by the Minister should be tried out in an effort to find the right answer'.

To this letter in *The Schoolmaster* there was a lively response from teachers. If we make the assumption that the letters printed were a representative selection of the letters received by the editor, and if we further assume that those who contribute letters to the correspondence columns of newspapers and periodicals are not so odd as to be unrepresentative of the general body, then the response to the proposals in the Bill was far from being a favourable one.

The Third Reading loomed ahead. Many members who had not quite realised how much support Follick and Pitman had mustered became alarmed at the possibility that the Simplified Spelling Bill might be passed. A few of them regarded it as a real threat to the structure of the English language. The supporters of the Bill were encouraged by the results of the Second Reading and rallied support for the forthcoming debate. Right up almost to the date fixed for the Third Reading there was considerable activity on both sides. Then suddenly, to the surprise of the public at large and even of the general body of parliamentary members, the Bill was withdrawn. There was a general feeling of disappointment among both supporters and opponents, particularly among those professionally engaged in education because the matter had brought education into the headlines and many were looking forward with great interest to another parliamentary debate. Having got so far, having shown such persistence over the years, why had Follick and Pitman apparently thrown up the sponge on the eve of victory? The full answer did not become apparent straight away. A compromise had been reached: the Ministry of Education would agree to the carrying out of experiments in schools provided that local authorities were in favour and that the right of parents to refuse to allow their children to be taught an unorthodox spelling was respected. Subsequent events showed that Follick and Pitman had withdrawn merely to better their advance, though Follick did not live to see how complete the victory was. If the Bill as drafted had reached the Statute Book, the Minister of Education would have had to do more than allow the i.t.a. experiment to go on, for the Bill provided that he should initiate other experiments than the Simplified Spelling one in order to find the right answer to the problem of teaching reading. As it was, though much preparation of opinion had still to be done and a considerable amount of teaching material had to be seen through its initial stages, the way was clear, with Government blessing, for the one proposed solution to be tested and there was no legal necessity for the Minister or anyone else to set up any investigation based on some contrary hypothesis.

For the sake of general efficiency a rational system of English spelling is, I believe, thoroughly desirable. As things now are, enormous amounts of teachers' time and energy are spent on defeating the attempts of generation after generation of children to spell the English language on reasonably logical lines. One of the members of Parliament in discussing the Simplified Spelling Bill said that our present forms of spelling were now tied up with snob-values. Veblen many years ago cited English spelling as a prime example of 'conspicuous waste', and although it is true that those who advocate a rational system of spelling are often thought of as cranks by those who have not studied the matter, there is a sufficient body of informed opinion at the present time to give an air of respectability to suggestions that English spelling might profitably be simplified.

What stands in the way of such a change? Most powerful of all is the idea that people who cannot spell in the accepted way are regarded as not fully literate and indeed, in circumstances as they are at present, it is difficult to regard poor spellers as fully literate. If they did not learn what took up so much of their time in the primary school, how many other things did they fail to learn? If they were in the habit of reading books, how could they fail to notice the accepted way of spelling the words they read?

Another reason for the obdurate nature of our present system of spelling is that the forms of written language are deeply imbedded in our intellectual and emotional lives. The familiar forms of the printed word are part of our experience; they have a permanence in our minds that is part of the experience of literature. This is particularly true of poetry. One of Shakespeare's sonnets written in shorthand would not look like what we know it to be even if we were fluent readers of shorthand. And what about the Bible? There are people who would regard it as sacrilege to write the Lord's Prayer in shorthand.

A third obstacle to changes in our spelling is sheer ignorance. Although Sir Walter Raleigh spelt his name in nearly twenty different ways–and all of them right–nowadays we are so used to particular ways of writing words that only one way seems right. Many people shudder at the sight of 'thru' for 'through'; the latter form has thru long usage been established as the natural form; to go against it is to interfere with natural law.

Some minor reasons are: It is thought by some that to make spelling simpler is to take away a much needed discipline from education; others think that if we rationalised our spelling we should lose some of the historical associations of words because our spelling is a mixture of the phonetic and the etymological. Yet who would lose much history from the dropping of the 'h' in *rhubarb*? Etymological accuracy would even be gained by dropping the 'g' in 'sovereign'. Again it is objected that the spoken language changes, so that if we modified the alphabet in such a way as to make it accurately represent the sounds of speech, we'd in the end be no better off and words like *through*, *knot* and *knee* are given as examples of words containing letters now silent that formerly represented sounds that were spoken.

We are concerned here with an alphabet to be used merely for the initial stage of teaching reading. Yet what I have said about the rationalisation of English spelling is very much to the point. Some of the objections to the Pitman scheme, as the Parliamentary debate showed, comes from the belief that i.t.a. is the thin edge of a wedge which may eventually be used to crack the foundations of our orthodox way of spelling. Furthermore, i.t.a. is itself a rationalisation of English spelling, and finally the main value of i.t.a. in my opinion lies in the possibility that it offers the possibility of a break-through to a rational system of spelling. True, Sir James Pitman disclaims any intention of revolutionising English spelling and I believe he would be satisfied to see i.t.a. accepted merely as a recognised teaching medium in schools, but, if it is to that degree accepted, a generation of children will grow up to whom the idea of a regularised spelling of English will not be alien. They may even develop a sentimental attachment to it because of its association with childhood days and so some of the obstacles to change may disappear automatically. The ingenuity of the Pitman compromise also is such that traditional orthography will present no reading difficulty to those who have learned to read i.t.a. This sketch of the future may well be optimistic, but these developments seem possible: they also seem to me highly desirable in a world which has shrunk so much with the increased speed and flexibility of communication.

I turn now to the i.t.a. investigations as they have so far been reported. The aim of the experimental design is 'to establish on an objective basis whether or not the use of i.t.a. for beginning reading produces improvements in children's attainments in reading and other school subjects (Downing: *The i.t.a. Reading Experiment*). The basic plan is to obtain reliable objective data for a valid assessment of the new medium by comparing at least 2,500 children using i.t.a. and a matched control group beginning reading with the traditional alphabet and spelling.

For the first phase of the investigation it was decided to use the most popular reading scheme in Britain, the *Janet and John* series. The whole series was printed in i.t.a. and many other books for the classroom library corner were reprinted in the new medium. By the end of 1962 over 200 titles were available in i.t.a.–a staggering figure. It is safe to say that no educational experiment of the kind has ever had such resources at its disposal. Besides these books, teaching apparatus has been manufactured and teachers themselves have created new material.

At the beginning of 1961, education authorities in different areas of Britain were asked to co-operate. Meetings of head teachers were held and before the meetings each head teacher received a pamphlet, *The Augmented Roman Alphabet–a new two-stage method of teaching children to read* (Downing, 1961). Twenty-one schools were selected for the introduction of i.t.a. and other schools were chosen to provide control classes using ordinary methods and materials. The teachers who were to work with i.t.a. were given two separate day-sessions in which they were introduced to the new alphabet and discussed how the new medium would affect the teaching of reading, writing and spelling. Between the two days the teachers had to carry out a practice assignment in writing i.t.a. The parents of the children were not neglected. Each parent received a booklet called *How your Children are being taught to read by the Augmented Roman Alphabet Method* (Downing, 1961) and discussions took place at Parent-Teacher meetings. The parents were also encouraged to buy i.t.a. books from the schools and to borrow them from public libraries. They were told, too, not to keep conventionally printed books away from the children because these books provided additional support and also necessary experiences of 'grown-up writing'.

All these preparations would obviously have given a great advantage to the i.t.a. schools if similar work had not been done with the teachers were pupils were to provide the control group. So these teachers also were given refresher courses and attended meetings to discuss the research.

At the end of the first year the control group was given the orthodox version of the Schonell Graded Word Reading Test and the experimental group was given the same test transliterated into i.t.a. The i.t.a. group were shown to be significantly superior in these tests—not unexpectedly, I think. Why should not regularly spelt words be easier to read than irregularly spelt ones? In the i.t.a. version of the Schonell test which was given to the experimental group all the words were by definition regularly spelt. Much more to the point are the results of testing whether children taught i.t.a. are able to transfer to traditional orthography. The hypothesis to be tested was whether pupils who had first learned with i.t.a. would read traditional orthography with significantly greater speed, accuracy and comprehension than pupils who had not used i.t.a. in the initial stages. To test this hypothesis 146 pupils who had been having i.t.a. lessons for eighteen months and 190 pupils from the control group were given the orthodox version of the Neale Analysis of Reading Ability test. At this time rather less than half of the i.t.a. children had been transferred to orthodox books in class. This Neale test produces measures of speed, accuracy and comprehension. In this test the i.t.a. children were not *significantly* (in the statistical sense) superior in speed of reading orthodox print but 'showed a tendency' towards faster reading. On the other hand they were shown to be significantly superior in both accuracy and comprehension.

These are highly satisfactory results to those who start with a bias in favour of i.t.a. They have encouraged Sir James Pitman to the extent of declaring that he will be surprised if within three years–from 1964–the majority of schools are not using i.t.a.

The i.t.a. experiments have not been without their critics both in the teaching profession and outside it. On the one hand there have been criticisms from linguists. Dr. Axel Wijk of the University of Stockholm, for example, wrote a pamphlet denouncing the new alphabet as phonetically unsound and there have been various criticisms in the correspondence columns of the educational press of the manner in which the investigation has been planned. As a result of some of these criticisms Mr. Downing was moved to write in the *Times Educational Supplement* (18th October), 1963):

The disappointment of advocates of 'phonics' as the method to teach reading upon the discovery that we are not collecting 'proof' of the value of 'phonics' is matched only by the distress of the spelling reformers when they find that i.t.a. is not a 'phonic' or 'phonetic' alphabet but an 'initial teaching alphabet' designed to help children to learn to read the traditional alphabet and spelling of English with greater accuracy and comprehension. Actually most teachers in our experiment are eclectic in their approach.

The Pitman alphabet is an easy target for those who advocate a simplification of English spelling on purely phonetic principles; even the fundamental rule of one symbol for each 'sound' is not always observed. If a precise guide to the pronunciation of English is wanted, then i.t.a. is not the place to look for it. What i.t.a. does is to provide in print a guide to the sounds of the spoken word *without confusion*. And it does this without so greatly altering the appearance of print as to make currently orthodox print very difficult to read. The child or adult who learns through the medium of i.t.a. becomes literate in orthodox print too.

In the more immediate field of teaching reading to English-speaking children, the regular spelling of i.t.a. has enormous advantages. Up to now, as we have seen, the irregularity of English spelling has been one of the prime causes of confusion in theory and confusion of practice. It has been argued that letters are of no importance in early reading experiences; it has been argued that a knowledge of letters must necessarily precede any reading experience whatsoever; children have been theoretically required to 'see' whole sentences at a glance before they have seen letters; vocabularies of reading books have been 'scientifically' controlled almost out of existence altogether in a most unscientific manner; and on the other hand letters have sometimes been to such an extent controlled that word-meanings have disappeared from the reading matter altogether: *ab, eb, ib, ob, ub.*

Sir James Pitman's move in getting i.t.a. into schools has the simplicity–once the implications are seen–of a brilliant move in chess; it accomplishes so many things at one stroke:

1. The controversy between look-and-say and phonics no longer seems important because i.t.a., though not by the strictest standards a *phonetic* print, is on account of its regularity a *phonic* print and is therefore the kind of print that 'phonics' needs. On the other hand the look and say teacher will, with i.t.a., be using material which does not confuse the child, at the i.t.a. stage anyway, who must necessarily learn by way of a process of visual and auditory analysis.

2. There is no longer any necessity for going through the difficult process of selecting regularly spelt words for early teaching material with the unfortunate results that have attended most of these efforts.

3. There is no need with i.t.a. to restrict the vocabulary as severely to a few frequently repeated 'sight' words–a process which so often results in reading material that is not much more meaningful than that which was found in books containing such sentences as *Can a pig jig in a wig?*

4. At the same time i.t.a. will free the shackles of English spelling and it becomes possible to look forward with more confidence to a time when English spelling is more in keeping with the position of English as the main international language in a telecommunicative world.

It would be very odd, however, if there were no flies in the ointment. It may be remembered that according to one of the reports on similar experiments in America in the 19th century very few of the pupils brought up on i.t.a. were good spellers and the two systems of spelling set up 'permanent confusion' in the minds of the learners. It is not enough for the investigators at the present stage of the investigation to suggest that the i.t.a. pupils were as accurate spellers as the control group because the theory behind the *Janet and John* series is not one which is likely in practice to inculcate accuracy in spelling at the early stages. Pupils who read 'ocvcglome' as 'aeroplane' are not perceiving the word with the accuracy necessary for correct spelling. So it may be that i.t.a. pupils will for some time at least be less accurate spellers of orthodox forms than pupils taught to read by a letter-based method.

The research which is now being conducted into the value of i.t.a. is much less impressive than the idea of i.t.a. itself. It has all the appearance of being planned to persuade public opinion to accept i.t.a. rather than to discover the truth. Those who have followed my argument about the process of learning to read in a previous chapter will, even if they disagree with my reasoning, find it easy to understand why I believe that the choice of look-and-say books as the basis of the investigation biased the results in favour of i.t.a. from the outset. It would have been rather more difficult to show that i.t.a. pupils were superior in reading ability to pupils taught by a letter-based method. On the other hand an experiment designed to test i.t.a. against one of the more modern letter-based methods, e.g., D. H. Stott's *Programmed Reading Kit* or the *Royal Road Readers*, would not have had so great an impact

upon teacher and public opinion even if i.t.a. had proved
to be superior because that teaching material is not so
widely used as is the *Janet and John* series. That i.t.a.
should at some time be compared with a phonically graded
scheme in orthodox print has been suggested by Downing.
If, however, i.t.a. is shown to be a sweeping success on the
Janet and John level, the comparison between it and other
methods will be so small a thing that, whether the result
favours i.t.a. or not, it will not, in all likelihood, be regarded
as much more than of academic interest. It is probably
of academic interest, too, that when Downing refers to
the necessity of comparing i.t.a. with material from which
irregularly spelt words are excluded at the early stages,
he does so in a way which must surprise anyone familiar
with the history of methods of teaching reading.

Inconsistently spelt words could be abolished from early
books as is recommended by Bloomfield and Barnhart (1961).
Even though this may mean using material such as 'Nan can
fan Dan. Can Dan fan Nan? Dan can fan Nan', it is an alternative which needs to be explored in comparison with i.t.a.

What a proliferating series of half-truths have we here!
Let's Read (1961) did indeed suggest the omission of
irregularly spelt words at the early stages. But so too
have nearly all phonic readers of all kinds for the past 150
years. Is the intention to suggest that Bloomfield and
Barnhart are the most up-to-date advocates of such a
scheme? Bloomfield had been dead for a number of years
in 1961 and Barnhart was merely seeing into print with
some additions the scheme which Bloomfield had outlined
in 1942 but had failed to find a publisher for. Not sur-
prisingly, because the sentences quoted were typical,
publication became possible only by means of a grant from

the Ford Foundation. Or is it intended to suggest that the
only result of omitting irregularly spelt words at the early
stages is to produce sentences like *Nan can fan Dan*,?
But that is the very thing that J. C. Daniels and I were
struggling against ten years ago.

The results achieved by means of i.t.a. so far as they
have been reported to date do not seem to have been
superior to those that were reported of the 'phonic word
method' in *Progress in Reading* and *Progress in Reading in
the Infant School*. Where i.t.a. has a certain advantage is
once they have changed to i.t.a. teachers do not have to
change their methods. This is a point made with great
conviction by Sir James Pitman. I see here, however, a
disadvantage that outweighs the advantage, for it means
that teachers need do no fundamental re-thinking of the
processes of reading.

The results achieved by the i.t.a. method cannot be
regarded as striking by those who have read *Progress in
Reading* and *Progress in Reading in the Infant School* with
some care. Indeed in a statistical analysis yet to be published, in which he was able to compare the achievement
of the infants investigated in the latter report with the
infants in the i.t.a. experimental groups, J. C. Daniels
found that the i.t.a. children were significantly inferior in
reading achievement to those in the 'phonic words method'
infant investigation. Why should this be so? No doubt this
may be found worthy of investigation. Two reasons
immediately suggest themselves and ought perhaps to be
taken into account if any investigation is to be made into
this question:

1. Children taught by i.t.a. are living in a lettered world
which has special confusions. They see around them on

breakfast cereal packets, ice-cream cartons, in books, comics and newspapers nothing but traditional orthography and in school they are given books which have been deliberately separated from their everyday visual experience even while kept as similar as possible. The assumption is that the vague perception which does not notice these differences is all that young children are capable of. This assumption does not seem to hold good against the experimental work reported in *Reading and the Psychology of Perception*.

2. The manner in which i.t.a. has been introduced has had the effect of deflecting the attention of the teachers concerned from some of the fundamental problems of reading. It is argued that one of the advantages of i.t.a. is that a teacher need not change her method—only the material needs to be changed. This is as much as to say that she need not re-examine her ideas. The use of the *Janet and John* readers as teaching material indicates that the i.t.a. proponents have either rejected or not thought important the facts about perception which the advocates of the 'phonic word method' regarded as fundamental. It may well be, then, that the greater success of the latter method is also due to a re-thinking of ideas on the part of the teachers who used it, for at that time teachers who used the 'phonic word method' in infant schools met with so much criticism that in the main they had to equip themselves with the ideology of the method.

Chapter Nine

FINALLY

THE writing of this book has been largely a matter of exclusion. Many names have been mentioned, but many more left out. Some reading experts whose names appear in nearly every bibliography about reading are not mentioned in this book or receive only a passing reference. The reason for this is that I have been concerned with the *movement* of ideas and not many of the writers whose names are most familiar to students of reading have given a new direction to the trends of thought on this subject. Their reputations have been due rather to the diligence with which they have buttressed orthodox opinion. Indeed one of the striking things about the literature on reading is it repetitiousness. This is truer of American work than of English. In England, where staffs of universities and training colleges are not under strong pressure to keep on publishing, two or three years may elapse between the publication of one book on reading and the next; here the writing on reading consists mostly of short simple articles in teachers' journals or longer articles in the more abstruse periodicals giving technical reports on research. In America, however, where academic eminence is highly correlated with the number of words published, lengthy books on reading appear so frequently that the uninitiated may well doubt whether there can be so much new to be said about reading as to justify another 150,000 or 200,000 word book on the subject. If he looks at a random half-dozen of these books, he is likely to find his doubt justified.

M

The chances are that that half-dozen will be so much alike that he will wonder why five of them ever came to be published. Several reasons suggest themselves. Some of the books are published to give backing to sets of elementary school readers bearing the same author's name; some are published to bring a prestige name into the publisher's list; a few because the publishers feel that they have discovered a manuscript with something new to say on this well-worn subject. And no doubt every one of them is published in the hope that it will become a college textbook for students training to be teachers.

The basic ingredients of nearly all these books, however, were already in Huey's book of 1908. Nearly all the books published on this subject in America since then have done little more than put into different words what Huey had already said, with varying emphases, a greater number of references and longer bibliographies in which Huey's name appears with increasing rarity. I think it is in this matter of references and bibliographies that we find the most substantial reason for the great number of books published on the teaching of reading. Research reports continue to pour from the presses. So much so that it has been found necessary every few years to publish guides to research on reading and two or three years ago one of the big foundations ear-marked a considerable number of dollars in order to enable a team of research-workers to carry out an elaborate programme of research into research on reading. One of the effects of all this activity is to put books on reading out of date, or apparently out of date, fairly quickly. The author of a book is unlikely to be able to make any reference to a research report which was still in the press when his book was published. That is some-

thing the author of one of next year's books will be able
to do. So the books continue to appear full of ideas half a
century old but as up to date as possible with their
references and bibliographies. Perhaps I am giving the
impression that research into reading during the past
fifty years has been singularly unprofitable. This is an
impression I am reluctant to give, but there is very little
I can do about it, for in some years of reading on this
subject I came across nothing in the way of research which
I felt showed something that a mixture of keen observation
and shrewd commonsense could not have found out—
except perhaps the clever photography of Buswell and a
few others which produced much more accurate records
of eye-movements in reading than had existed before.

Although the vast amount of research that had been
carried out, has stimulated a constant flow of general
surveys of the state of knowledge about reading, there has
been little sign that the results of research have been
fairly reflected either in these summaries or in the teaching
that goes on in American schools. At any rate Flesch listed
a substantial number of pieces of research that he regarded
as significant but that had been ignored or only rather
slightingly referred to in most of the general books on
reading, and Fries put in emphatic italics the statement that
he had found no evidence that the findings of research had
had much effect upon the practices of advice that was
being given to teachers.

There is undoubtedly something of a mystery about
all this. A considerable number of experiments have
shown that phonic methods of one kind or another are
more successful than non-letter-based methods of teaching
reading, but they are easily dismissed by those who wish

to dismiss them. It is merely a matter of saying that these methods produce barkers at print who do not understand, and show no interest in understanding, what they are barking at. A boy of nearly twelve who had failed to learn to read by conventional methods to the extent of being unable to recognise any printed word but his own name was taught to read simple words like *man*, *sand* and *and* within an hour. A day or two later he was stumbling his way through simple sentences. But was this accepted as possibly an indication that his initial success was due to his being taught something about what letters *meant*? No. It was all explained away by the statement that he must have been caught just when he was ready!

And what about the numerous inconsistencies? We have Huey saying that the child may well be given alphabet blocks to play with and that the parent need never fear that a knowledge of letters will stand in the way of the child's progress in reading, but a chapter or two further on, writing as though the last thing a child should learn is what the letters stand for. We find Schonell in *Backwardness in the Basic Subjects* advocating in early reading material the use of words of as different shape as possible, but, in his own reading-books, rejecting that principle out of hand. And Duncan in his *Backwardness in Reading* advocates the direct linking of the printed word-pattern with meaning 'without the interpolation of sound'; yet in the *Duncan Readers* there is a high phonic content.

What is the explanation of these inconsistencies?

It is no answer to imply, as Flesch does, that all educationists are naïve. Nor is it an answer to point to statistical evidence of the superiority of one method or another. But it is at least part of an answer to say that the rejection of

both alphabetic and phonic methods was part of the reaction against the drill methods of the 19th century. It can
be said indeed that when education became child-centred,
less attention was paid to the nature of the subject the
child was learning. 'We teach children not subjects,'
became one of the educational platitudes. And yet the
platitude was grammatically ambiguous. Can you teach a
child without teaching him something? Alphabetic and
phonic methods had become associated with rows and
rows of children mouthing letters and syllables. This
association has probably been weakened in the last few
years but it is disappearing slowly.

But perhaps the most substantial reason for the rejection
of letters is to be found among the children themselves.
The normally alert child will not wait for a well-thought
out scheme to get under way. While the teacher is patiently
trying to get the child to understand why *man* is printed
as it is, the child is 'reading' *ice-cream, bicycle* and *aeroplane*
with no apparent difficulty. For the child, like the adult,
reads different words in different ways. He will patiently
work his way through the letters and produce the word
when required to do so by the teacher, but he will just
as often 'read' a word that he recognises by this or that
charactistic whether of outline or of individual letter. In
fact the child mixes his methods of word recognition.
There is a very strong case then for saying that 'mixed
methods' follow the child's natural tendencies. Does this
mean that Schonell was right in suggesting the use of words
of as many different shapes as possible in early reading
material? I think not. By all means the child should be
allowed to experiment with reading and should have
available books with interesting pictures and brief texts

through which he may browse in search of words that he thinks he can read. But at the same time there should be available to him books designed to teach him why the letters are there in the particular order on the page in front of him. It is from such books that he is most likely to acquire the basic knowledge necessary for progress towards full reading ability—that is, insight into what the letters *mean*.

POSTSCRIPT

AFTER this book had reached the production stage, considerable publicity was given in England to the theory and method
of Glenn J. Doman of Philadelphia. The *Sunday Mirror* in
October and November, 1964 published a series of articles
on his book *Teach Your Baby to Read* (Cape, London) 1965,
and invited parents of two-year-old children to join in an
experiment in teaching these very young children to read.
There is nothing revolutionary about the method. It is indeed
the most orthodox of the look-and-say methods. The only
differences are that the print is bigger, the child is younger,
and Mr. Doman insists that the younger a child begins to learn
the easier it is for him.

The 'babies' begin by learning to recognise the words
'mummy' and 'daddy' as whole words, these words being
printed in large lower-case letters in red ink on cards. The
first lessons last only a minute or two. When they have learned
to recognise those two words, the 'babies' then go on to learn
to recognise a number of words called the 'self' words, i.e. the
names of various parts of their bodies. They go on to a 'book'
and, later, learn the alphabet.

The most interesting thing about this latest development is
that it shows so extreme a reaction against the idea that children
will learn to read when they are ready and not before. It will be
remembered that seventy years or so ago John Dewey, who
was against a book-dominated education for the early years,
seriously asserted that nine or ten was the best age for children
to begin to learn to read and that much of the thinking about
reading during the past three or four decades has been dominated by Dolch's insufficiently proved assertion that a child
must have a mental age of seven before he can be expected to
learn to read.

A good critical estimate of 'reading readiness' is to be found in a chapter by Glenn McCracken in *To-morrow's Illiterates* (Little, Brown, Boston, 1961). An account of the development of perception of abstract figures, words, and letters with 'babies' is given in my own *Reading and the Psychology of Perception* and an excellent account of how a 'baby' learned to read is given in Ronald Morris's *Success and Failure in Learning to Read* (Oldbourne, London, 1963).

English parents would do well, I think, to remember that in America those children who do not attend a kindergarten start school a year later than English children and that the considerable amount of criticism of school methods in America have made many parents impatient with the orthodox reading methods in American schools. It would be well, too, for parents who try to teach their babies to read to be aware that the word-recognition stage is a very easy one. The trial of the teacher's patience comes when she is trying to get the child to understand what the letters are there for. Children will appear to be able to read long before they are actually able to do so in the full sense of the word.

BIBLIOGRAPHICAL NOTE

So much has been written, and is being written, about the teaching of reading that in America it has been found necessary to publish a bibliographical volume on this topic every few years. The compiler is A. E. Traxler with various collaborators and the publishers are the Educational Records Bulletin, N.Y. The following have so far been published.

Ten Years of Reading Research. 1941.
Another Five Years of Research in Reading. 1946.
Eight More Years of Research in Reading. 1955.
Research in Reading during another Four Years. 1960.

Other bibliographies appear fairly regularly in *The Reading Teacher* published by the International Reading Association at Newark, Delaware.

There are 744 column inches under the heading 'Reading' in the 1960 edition of the *Encyclopedia of Educational Research* (Macmillan, New York).

As a reasonably detailed, but not overloaded, survey of research and ideas in this field up to the date of its publication I recommend Anderson and Dearborn's *The Psychology of Teaching Reading*.

Although I have said in this book that most of the experts on reading during this century have said hardly anything that Huey did not say or imply in 1908, the work of Gates, Gray and Witty in America and Schonell in England can hardly be neglected by those who wish to be knowledgeable about this subject. In the case of Gray it is necessary to note that the 1960 edition of *On Their Own in Reading* is so different from that of 1948 that it really ought to have a different title. The first chapter of Schonell's *Psychology and Teaching of Reading* and the section on 'How Children Recognise Words' in his *Backwardness in the Basic Subjects* inadvertently show in the briefest possible space how confused thinking had become about the process of perception in reading.

A fairly recent English book which shows more penetration of thought than is usual in books on reading is Morris's *Success and Failure in Reading*. This book also looks at past ideas about teaching reading in a critical and revealing way.

I have not put in the select bibliography below all the books referred to in the text. Where it seemed desirable I gave the essential publication details in the text itself. The books I have listed, however, are either key books in the history of reading or books which throw light on some particular aspect of reading theory. The exception is Anderson and Dearborn's which is included for the reason given above.

SELECT BIBLIOGRAPHY

Anderson, I. F. and Dearborn, W. F. *The Psychology of Teaching Reading* (Ronald Press, N.Y.) 1952.

Dale, N., *On the Teaching of English Reading* (Dent, London) 1898.

Diack H. *Reading and the Psychology of Perception* (Ray Palmer, formerly Peter Skinner, Nottingham) 1961, (Philosophical Library, N.Y.) 1961.

Flesch, R., *Why Johnny Can't Read* (Harper, N.Y.) 1955.

Fries, C. C., *Linguistics and Reading* (Holt Rinenart, N.Y.) 1963.

Gates, A. I., *The Improvement of Reading* (Macmillan, N.Y.) 1947.

Gray, W. S., *The Teaching of Reading and Writing* (UNESCO, Paris) 1956.

——*On Their Own in Reading* (Scott Foresman, Chicago) 1948, Second Edition, 1960.

Huey, E. B., *The Psychology and Pedagogy of Reading* (Macmillan, N.Y.) 1908.

Jagger, J. H., *The Sentence Method of Teaching Reading* (Grant, London) 1929.

Morris. R., *Success and Failure in Learning to Read* (Oldbourne, London) 1963.

Schonell, F. J., *The Psychology and Teaching of Reading* (Oliver and Boyd, Edinburgh) 1945.

—— *Backwardness in the Basic Subjects* (Oliver and Boyd, Edinburgh) 1942.

Terman, S. and Walcutt, C. C., *Reading : Chaos and Cure* (McGraw Hill, N.Y.) 1958.

Witty, P. A., *Reading in Modern Education* (Heath, Boston) 1949.

INDEX